The Fight Of My Life

My Journey to Freedom

Apostle Julia D. Ford

Published in the United States of America by ChosenButterflyPublishing LLC

www.cb-publishing.com

Cover design and photograph by BJ Shores for SMG Productions/ Shooterz Photos

ISBN 978-098316376-3

First Edition Printing

ChosenButterfly Publishing
P.O Box 515
Millville, NJ 08332

Printed In the United States of America
October 2012

For more information about this author please visit:
www.thefightofmylife.info

For bookings and speaking engagements email
jdfthegeneral@aol.com

Table Of Contents

Foreword...

This book is a powerful reflection of the "**FIGHT**" that is in Apostle Julia D. Ford. I count it a privilege and honor to be your husband and Pastor. You are indeed a "**FIGHTER**". I have seen you overcome many adversities only to come out very triumphantly. God has taught you how to stop warring against flesh & blood and to "**FIGHT**" the spirits that have been attacking you from childhood. It gives me great joy to have you by my side as my wife and in the work of the ministry. God is well pleased with the completion of your first book. Your passion and dedication to see others move beyond their own current lines of resistance is remarkable. Your ability to paint such a clear and vivid picture with your words will allow all readers to understand what is needed to overcome any obstacle in their lives. I am certain that every reader will be encouraged to examine their own lives and too will become equipped with the tools to "**FIGHT**" until they attain complete victory through Christ Jesus.

Congratulations on a well written testament of your life's journey to freedom. I know that this is just the beginning of many more books to come. Keep up the good "FIGHT" of faith Mighty Woman of God.

Proudly from my heart to yours,
Apostle Owen E. Ford, Jr.
Senior Pastor
True Love Church

Foreword...

Apostle Julia Ford is a woman of God that gets aggressive when it comes to launching out into the deep. Her ability to motivate herself makes her a dynamic motivator of others. I love her creativity and ingenuity when it comes to "Making Things Happen," and that is why I am so excited and enthusiastic about the release of this, her first book: "The Fight Of My Life - My Journey To Freedom."

Readers get ready as she shares her life and the amazing "roller coaster ride" along with the "round by round" battles that she endured to get to the level in God where she is today. As my spiritual daughter, I know and understand the Apostolic/Prophetic call on her life and her understanding of spiritual warfare, so believe me when she shares with you how Christ delivered her from being "*the victim*" into "*the Victor*" it's because she used weapons of warfare to drive the enemy out of her life.

This book is about the Fight of Her Life, but it is her goal for you to take the tactics and strategies she shares in this book along with the personal situations she journeyed through and make it your own. In other words, take the *"stuff"* she gives you in this book and use it to gain access to Freedom in your life with the *"stuff"* you're going through.

May the Power of God that set Apostle Julia free do the same for you....Get Aggressive!!!

I'm proud of you my spiritual daughter...

Apostle Alexander Wm. Thompson, Jr.
Ever Abundant Life Ministries, Founder/Sr. Pastor
AAT Power Ministries, Founder/CEO

Dedication....

Loving the Lord, the way that I do there's absolutely no possible way I could not dedicate this first milestone as a new author to Him FIRST. Father, thank you for believing in me, trusting in me and never letting me quit. THANK YOU FOR GIVING ME WHAT TO SAY ON THIS SIDE OF THE MOUNTAIN. I vow to never let you down.

To my God-fearing, amazing, handsome and supportive husband, Apostle Owen E. Ford, Jr. You are my husband, my king and my Pastor. Your unconditional love and teachings have allowed me to soar. I'm simply everything that I am because you love me!

To the 3 most awesome young adults that a mother could have; thank you for giving my life meaning, Owen III, Julian and Milan. You have filled my life with so much joy and laughter. Thank you for choosing me to be your mom right before you left heaven. I promise to make you proud of me.

To the absolute best church family this side of Heaven - True Love Church, thank you for loving me to back to life.

To the multi-talented photographer extraordinaire BJ Shores & Shooterz Photoz - thank you for capturing my vision at a moment's notice.

To my auntie Delaine Wilson, thanks so much for offering to help with my unknown project. You encouraged and motivated me to be the best me.

This Is It.....

Singing, ***"This is it! You can't mess with my mind anymore; This is it! I'm smarter see I've been here before, This is it! Its new day, I'm not afraid anymore, This is it! YES I BELIEVE, YES I BELIEVE, help me say...THIS IS IT!"*** I really thought this was just another great song by Kirk Franklin but actually it was the story of my life. The day I heard ***"This is it!"*** helped to put a lot of things into better perspective. In the beginning, it was just a new song that I finger-popped to the beat and smoothly bounced my head to the catchy tune, but it quickly became my declaration. Declaration: *a statement made by a party to a legal transaction. It is an announcement.* By the song's end I had begun to declare to myself, the world and mostly the devil....***THIS IS IT!***

There should come a time in everyone's life where running, hiding, ducking or even ignoring the enemy's attacks just gets old and tiring. The enemy comes to provoke and nag us into his battles. I do believe that our spiritual discernment should be sharp and prepared to be used. We shouldn't be quick to run into a battle against the enemy and his camp if we are ill-prepared. Spiritual discernment: *the quality of being able to grasp and comprehend what is hidden.* In other words you 'gotta know when to hold-em, know when to fold-em, know when to walk away and know when to run'. It's up to us as believers to know which battles to ***FIGHT***.

I had finally realized how sick and tired I had been of the enemy's attacks on me, my family and friends and even with those that deemed me as their enemy. Singing, ***THIS IS IT!*** was more than just words - the more I said it, the louder I became and the louder I became, the more I had become convinced....***THIS REALLY IS IT!*** This was the day I chose to serve divorce papers to the enemy. I no longer wanted to give him permission to torment my mind with the things of the past. I no longer wanted to stand by on the sidelines of my life watching the enemy co-sign to my twisted thoughts on my current mental state. Nor did I take too kindly to the threats he had tried to make against my future. He has even tried to send his cohorts 'the spirits of Fear and Dread' along to seal the deal. YES! This is the day I proudly announced ***"THIS IS IT!"***

My prayer for you today is to find your place called ***THIS IS IT!*** Don't ignore the signs the Lord is giving you to let you know that you are free to move into a better place. If you can't see yourself there yet, don't give up. I promise you, if you hold on and don't faint - your date to sign your declaration of freedom will come.

I pray through my trials and adversities you find your own way out of your current lines of resistance. This book will inspire and motivate you to finally come face-to-face with your past, make peace with your present - while preparing for your successful future. This book will help you get to the point of doing something about what has held you back for far too long. It's time for you beloved, to break through stagnant spirits that have come to entrap and hold you, never wanting to see you any more than what you are today. I'm living proof that which hasn't been able to kill me has truly made me stronger.... It's time to get dressed for the ring.....Soon the bell for each round will be rung.

~Round 1~

Ding... Ding...

School Fights

The Lord was training me up in the way I was supposed to go with a boy and while being jumped...

Every trained fighter has their personal reasons for choosing to make their living from professional fighting. Some may consider their life never really gave them a choice. In the midst of this grueling and often times physical, emotional and mentally-challenging profession, many have found a sense of peace and purpose. Through the barrage of jabs, body blows and upper cuts, fighters have been well-equipped to counter every attack their opponent launches through punches, blocking and defending themselves.

Fighters must show great fortitude and strength against the hand of the enemy - or whom he has deemed his enemy, only for the purpose of the fight. Every fighter knows that in order to beat any opponent, you must be a trained and finely-tuned, oiled machine as Adam Sandler was in the movie "The Water Boy" so poignantly-stated. A great amount of dedication, overwhelming determination and skill are required to turn a mediocre fighter into a winning champion.

How do prize fighters get their start? Do they wake up one morning and say that they want to be a fighter? I believe most fighters - especially the really good ones, never originally wanted to be a boxer or are lovers of a good fight. I believe life circumstances will throw you into its ring to see what you are made of. It wants you to acquire strong hands, a conditioned body and a sharp mind poised for attacks.

~If babies are hit, they will not hit back. However after a baby is hit once and are told or shown how to hit back, then they will~

Life's on-going boxing tournaments will keep you in match after match until the end of the day, when all of your opponents will start to look alike. These seemingly-endless matches were never designed for you to win them: their purpose is to make you fight back, to frustrate you so that you become unaware of what you are doing and to simply wear you out.

Many fighters did not know that they could fight, let alone win any of the matches in life. We all have to start somewhere.

If babies are hit, they will not hit back. However after babies are hit once and are told or shown how to hit back, then they will. Once the baby understands there's a reaction to their actions, the baby will no longer have to be prompted to hit back. Hitting someone back will now become an automatic response to being hit. Now a danger in that is once a child learns to hit back, it may be a challenge to get them to stop.

We tell our children to not allow themselves to be picked on or to be mistreated. What we fail to do at times as parents is to help our children discern the differences between immediate threats, versus our feelings being hurt. The end results are children who will eventually turn into adults who have not learned how to properly process what they are feeling. The children develop mixed emotions with mixed reactions.

I believe hitting back is a concept that was introduced to us by humans. Families and friends tell us we must defend ourselves in order to protect what belongs to us. Our cheering section will encourage us not to be intimidated: go after what is ours and make the enemy pay for putting their hands on us. Personally, I had to learn how to FIGHT so that I could survive.

The song writer said it best, *"Don't push me cause I'm close to the edge, I'm trying not to lose my head, it's like a jungle sometimes it makes me wonder how to keep from going under."* Then another verse says, *"A child is born with no state of mind, blind to the ways of mankind, God is smiling on you but He's frowning too because only God knows what you'll go through."*

I found out that I was close to the edge much of the time when growing up. Not because I wanted to be, but because of the adult situations I witnessed and was often times involved in. It's said that a child is a victim of their environment. This was the case in my life. However through the grace of God, that way of life for me changed for the better. I found that I was always on edge due to abuse and ill exchanges of words. With that, I discovered my lack of tolerance for foolishness as early as elementary school age.

It's interesting how fast a child matures when they are forced to grow up faster than they should. I never thought I was better than anyone else - I just had a better perspective on the realities of life. I knew that those happy families I saw on TV were the same shared sentiments in real life. I knew that a child's world mainly thrived off of interactions from mommy and daddy and when there is a void there - the child is left with feelings of rejection, hurt and a pain that they just can't seem to put into words.

It was a challenge for me to interact socially for a while. I was a little girl with big-girl issues on my mind. Can I go outside at recess and play without wondering if my father was going steal me away like a thief in the night? Would the house phone ring tonight with my father on the other end mad at me because he can hear the disdain in my voice towards him? Would the call end up with him and mommy arguing? Would my father come to the house to argue with my mom and then threaten to hit her while my super-hero uncle quietly stood outside of his vehicle holding his rifle?

Side bar: My super-hero uncle came like clockwork to save the day, each and every day. He definitely was a man of few words and you were advised not to cross the line he drew in the sand - especially when he smoked a cigarette and turned his hat to the side. I don't know how he managed to arrive always in the nick of time - and this was before beepers and cell phones existed! Whenever there was confusion, my super-hero uncle would tell my sister and me to stay behind him. I never knew what this was all about, but I learned what it meant to feel safe from harm.

He loved us as if we were his biological daughters. For that, I am and will forever be grateful. He took us out to the park, joked around with us and treated us like queens right alongside his own daughter. Whenever I was in his presence, fear and paranoia subsided. Whenever he knew my father was out of pocket, he was there. My mother was the baby of seven, so naturally that meant you had to go through six others to get to her. However with my super-hero uncle, the other five never had to step up because he took care of all of us.

He died suddenly; way too soon. His death left my sister and I exposed to our dysfunctional parental elements. I remembered feeling scared like never before. What if my father would try to come harm us and my uncle was no longer there? What if he this? What if he that? My mind would race constantly. When my super-hero uncle passed away I remembered feeling empty, lonely and scared - but grateful that I had an opportunity to experience his love, laughter and protection.

In fact now as I write, I am reminded that he was the model man I would later be in search of as my husband. Due to my father's theatrics, I knew I could never see myself married if my only option was to marry someone like him. I'm not calling my biological father a monster - I'm just saying the picture that he painted when I was a child had a certain demonic flavor to it that caused me to repel against any and everything that would even resemble him. With all that chaos, the Lord erased what could have led to years of negative, marital duplication and instead showed me just how a real man stands up. My super-hero uncle was not perfect and I am sure he had flaws just like the rest of us. I just found it challenging to locate any of them.

Because of the many stresses and terrors I faced in my personal life while in elementary school, I kept to myself. I only felt comfortable being quiet. I was perfectly fine with not making friends because I was highly embarrassed by the behavior of my parents and the things I had endured. At this age, children are trying to find and hopefully embrace their identity. I didn't have time. I was too busy trying to figure out my next escape route and concentrating on such things as wondering if the canned foods I had stashed in a bag under my bed would spoil, just in case I had to exit out of my bedroom window quickly.

I was totally prepared to handle the next parental disaster. I was in 6th grade and had not given much thought to flirting with boys. I did not notice a particular boy who was in love with me. He tried hard to get my attention in any way that he could, even if it meant taunting me. He was as annoying as a pesky fly. He placed himself in my presence on every opportunity that presented itself. I found his reason to do so quite irritating. He always had something new to show me or a joke to tell. If he found that I wasn't amused, he would then start to call me names or start talking about how my body looked. For some reason his comments would get my attention. That made him happy.

~The enemy wants us to be unfocused and inattentive when it comes to Godly things.~

The enemy is doing the exact same thing to God's children. He allows his demonic team to fly all around us, trying to keep us irritated and frustrated. The enemy wants us to be unfocused and inattentive when it comes to Godly things. He will use his demonic spirits to divert our attention. The enemy tries to find just the right combination of buttons to push that will set us off. Yes, it is his job to provoke you by any means necessary. He wants you confused and in his FIGHTS that are fixed for you to loose. He wants to set you up to fail and then have you blame God for the failure. Beloved, we are to be as wise as serpents and as harmless as doves. Don't trip off of the first sign of a threat from the enemy. Be spirit-led in how you desire to bring closure to your hurt and pain.

Finally, the words of the young boy exasperated me. When he noticed that I was ready to flare-up, he then started to lightly tag me in the face, then hit my arm while verbally-taunting me. Yes I saw red and it was not due to the color of the blood Jesus shed. This kid thought what he was doing was funny and he was relentless. He thought he would harass me enough to chase him. I refused.

Finally the lunch bell rang and it was time to line up and go inside school for the second half of our day. He gave up, due to exhaustion. He bent over to try and catch his breath from running and laughing. I waited patiently in line. What happens to a young elementary school girl that feels she doesn't have anything to lose? She walked right over to him while the teacher poised to take the kids inside; swung her right hand to connect to his jaw, then her left hand flew to connect to the other side of his face and then she pushed him down, sat on his chest and kept hitting him until a male teacher picked her up off of him.

Never call someone out for a FIGHT if you are not prepared for their answer. You never know what is going on in the lives and minds of people. Everyone's tolerance for torment is different - people snap when they are pushed to their edge. As people of God we must only go to the edges of people's lives to save them, not to push them over. My mother was called. I really was unconcerned. When she arrived she later told me that she thought I was the one who was hurt - she was so upset on her way to the school because a boy had put his hands on her baby girl.

Well, when she got there he was on one side of the principal's office sitting on a bench holding ice on his eye - I was on the other side rolling my eyes hard at him. My mother stopped in her tracks and the look on her face was priceless. It took everything inside of her to keep from laughing. I was called into the office with my mother and principal.

The anointing on my life to be an Apostle and to do first work was ever-present then. The principal suggested my mom arrange for me to take boxing lessons or something. She stated that she'd never had a girl in her office for beating up a boy. When we were brought into the meeting with both parents and the principal, it was revealed that he really had a crush on me. He said he didn't know how to talk to me because I kept ignoring his jokes. *Honestly he wasn't even funny.*

People of God, the enemy will always get upset when you don't laugh at his jokes or demonic antics. Tell him it's not even funny. My mother laughed at me for about a week and I didn't get punished at school or home.

When the enemy knows you or your victory, he will do his best to come back to steal it away. The FIGHT with the boy was the first time I had ever laid hands on anyone. I was not sure of what I was doing: I just knew I wanted him to stop what I thought to be harassment. *I must admit once my fist made contact, I wanted to keep hitting him.* Every punch I threw was a great tension reliever. I did not know why I hadn't thought of this before. When the thought came across my mind, I wondered if that was how my father felt when he would hit me.

The enemy will always spread rumors about you and cause people to conspire against you. When you have a victory, the enemy will always try to throw his cohorts in the ring to go after you next. Taunting and telling you that you cannot take this person down. My FIGHT and its victory was simply a blessed punch.

Five girls in my class held secret counsel against me for about a week. I did not understand why, considering the fact that I did not talk to any of them. We didn't have anything in common, so why would they have fought against me? FYI Beloved - we can often times feel like groups are against us, as we are the children of God. Why is the enemy after me? What did I do to him? **Listen, toughen up**! Know that you can lie in bed all day and not speak to anyone and the enemy would still seek to cause your demise. He comes to steal, kill and destroy. He wants all of the people who are professing Christ as their Lord and Savior to become tired with the cares of this life. He wants to frustrate you and make you quit on all of the things of God. Don't be a 'punk-Christian'. Stand up and FIGHT the good FIGHT the way the word of God tells us too. Your season of being a whiney Christian is over. ***You are more than a conqueror through Christ Jesus!***

So these young ladies, who proudly wore the title of the school-girl bullies, surrounded me one day during lunch. They surrounded the table in such a way that didn't bring attention to the threats and taunts they were actively initiating against me. They never really gave me a chance to defend myself verbally against the verbal accusations they had brought before me.

Beloved, the enemy is the accuser of the brethren. His job is to go to God and accuse you of doing everything that's against the God you are proclaiming to serve. The Bible says to agree with your adversary quickly. Well I didn't know this at this particular time. All I knew was that I was tired of these girls and I wanted them to leave me alone. I still had lunch and recess to get through. I excused myself and walked to the bathroom.

Nothing will tick the enemy off more than when he is ignored. He doesn't leave, he's just gets ticked-off. I knew I didn't have to use the bathroom and I didn't have any girlfriends to walk with me to the bathroom. As soon as I left the table I instinctively knew they would follow me.

I looked back as I walked and yes, there they were. I did not have any plans on how to handle them, what to say or not to say. I just knew that fear was not an option and I had already been through too many personal issues to let these girls win at my expense.

Two steps into the bathroom, away from the lunch lady's view, I heard the ring leader call my name as if she had given birth to me. I turned to face her, but I did not answer her. She kept asking who I thought I was, leaving the lunch table without permission. She said she had not given me permission to go anywhere. Then I saw her fist ball up and she swung at me. The Matrix movie was not yet created, but I promise you - I moved just as swiftly as Neo when he realized he was the one they were looking for. She tried to hit me several times, all to no avail. Two more girls out of the five tried to hit me as well. They made no contact with their hits or punches. Complete misses!

I got tired of simply ducking their awkward attempts at punching. I knew that if I didn't do something great, I would have to look forward to another meeting in the ladies room. I threw a couple of punches. Another one of the girls tried to grab me to hold me so the others could hit me. That too failed. Soon as I felt the girl grab hold of me, I grabbed her ponytail and wrapped my hand around it. I held on to it long and hard. I was prepared to make her my example of why they should have left me alone. With my hand secured around her ponytail - I kicked one of the bathroom stalls in and pushed her head into the toilet a couple of times, then I pulled her up and banged her head against the metal-stall dividers.

I just wanted her to hurt outside as much as I was hurting inside. I knew I had to make her an example and I knew whatever I was going to do, I had to do it quickly. I did not want to experience a repeat of the fear and terror these girls were threatening me with. I was angry because through their taunts, I had refused to give them a reply, hoping by doing so they would just leave me be. Yet they felt entitled to provoke me to give them a response. The only answer I could give was the sweet sounds of my wrath. I found that I was not much of a conversationalist.

However when I found myself in a position of threat, I was able to muster up enough strength to speak their language, punch, kick and bang, right in the face. These girls actually felt they were going to get away with being mean, nasty and hateful to me. Honestly, they probably would have if they had not backed me into a corner. I only had one way out of that bathroom and I had to make a decision on how I was going to exit. I wasn't trying to be another Rocky Balboa - I just wanted to feel safe in the place where I was being sent to learn.

I didn't feel comfortable talking to the adult staff that was there because the adults in my personal life did nothing to stop the chaos and confusion there - why would I expect them to help me here? The fight only stopped because I stopped it. No one came in because the adults were not paying attention.

A lot of things will and do happen in our lives because those we have entrusted to care for us have failed to pay attention to details. Had the adults noticed that I was a loner from the beginning, they would have thought it odd for the group of girls to have randomly-approached me at the lunch table. Had the adults on duty known these groups of girls were trouble-makers, they would have known to monitor them a lot more closely.

~A lot of things will and do happen in our lives because those we have been entrusted to care for us, have failed to pay attention to details.~

As children of God, we must pay attention to details. It will allow us to know what is out of sync within ourselves and the things of God. God will sound the alarm many times on our behalf. He never wants us ignorant of the enemy's devices. We don't pay close attention to his movement throughout our lives, until it's six-hours past the trumpet alarmed and the enemy that was afar, is now right in our midst. Paying close attention to detail goes hand-in-hand with being spirit-led. Don't let the enemy foil you into thinking that details and close observation are not necessary. The Bible says that the Eyes of the Lord are in every place. He wants us to pay attention to detail because He pays attention to detail.

I promise you that when this FIGHT was over, I heard DING! DING! I knew I had won this round. I didn't leave school prideful or cocky - just confident. A couple of the girls left with headaches and the toilet girl needed a couple of stitches. We all got suspended for a couple of days. It was official, **I could FIGHT.**

You would be amazed at what you can do if given the tools to do so. It seems like creative juices flow a little better with deadlines and pressure. Let it be a healthy pressure to get you out of your comfort zone. Let your cheering section consist of Godly angels waving you on saying, "you can do it". Don't be led into FIGHTS for prideful gain. The Bible gives us a warning about that type of behavior and mindset. It says pride goes before destruction. So my caution beloved, is not to allow the mere fact of winning a FIGHT cause you a stumble and fall. Know that your purpose is pursuing you and that your destiny awaits you.

~Round 2~

Parental Dysfunction

Though my father and mother forsake me, the LORD will receive me.
Psalms 27:10 NIV

Psalms 27:10 NIV is a powerful scripture. *"Though my father and mother forsake me, the LORD will receive me."* The word "forsake" in this text is "AZAB." It means to be deserted, to depart from, leave behind, neglect. It is kind of disturbing to think that a parent could actually do any of these things to a child that was conceived by them.

Why would God warn us of this through His word? Why would He feel the need to inform us that this could be our lot in life? Why would God allow this to happen through parents? Didn't He know that we would grow up to believe that our parents are Superheroes and that they could do no wrong in our eyes? Didn't He know that children have a genuine innocence in the way they view their parents? Is it possible for a parent to just walk away from a child, or to neglect them and their needs? Apparently this is a possibility within every parent.

We don't know the plethora of reasons why people do what they do. Or how they could be at peace with themselves knowing that they have probably caused emotional and physical harm to a life they helped bring into the world. Instead of dwelling on the negative, I choose to find a solution - a way out.

The enemy would just love for the people of God to wallow in unforgiveness and hate towards our parents for the wrong doing we've felt they have committed. Some children will turn to drugs/alcohol - some to sex, some to a life of crime. Some will choose to just check out of reality. However, God is so kind. He knows the ending before the beginning. He knows exactly which parents will lead their babies on the road to destruction and which parents will make sure that their babies are given every opportunity to succeed, while making sure they are rooted and grounded in His word.

Beloved, God has already made ways of escape for us to get through the times of rejection we feel are a result of parents leaving and abandoning us. Many of us will eventually find out the real truth about mommy and daddy - and our world may come crashing down all around us with deafening sounds. We as adults must understand that our parents are humans with faults.

1 Corinthian 10:13 NIV says: *"No temptation has overtaken you except what is common to mankind. And God is faithful; he will not let you be tempted beyond what you can bear. But when you are tempted, he will also provide a way out so that you can endure it."*

The spirit of memory-recall would like for you to stay in those moments of hurt, pain, shame, guilt and blame. Those time periods when your parents were being demonically-used to bring harm to you, physically or emotionally. This spirit doesn't want you to forget what you felt when those things were happening to you - no matter how much you grow physically, emotionally and spiritually. This spirit wants to keep you at the age where you were hurt the most.

The spirit of memory-recall wants to control your every emotion and wants you to make decisions based on *how you feel*. Memory-recall never wants to be forgotten. So instead of forgetting and moving on, we tend to look for outlets that will be a temporary comfort to us.

~ God has already given you an exit strategy~

But know that God has already given you an exit strategy. His word tells us that when we are tempted by ungodly things, He the Lord will provide a way of escape; in other words, a way out for you. I believe that the cartoon character 'Snaggle Puss' said it best, "EXIT STAGE LEFT." Stage left for most of us is a place of safety and peace. If that's what you need right about now Beloved - then get to stepping to Stage Left. Some of us may have experienced rough, violent, abusive childhoods and it was in these times the Lord was strengthening us for His Kingdom Purpose. Many have endured name-calling, rejection, and neglect at the hands of our parents.

The Lord did not create us to be bitter by what we have had to endure, but to be ***better.*** It's not what you go through that defines you, but rather how you choose to respond to it that marks your place in history. Even when our parents knowingly or unknowingly hand us great big bowls of rejection topped with neglect, while encouraging us to sip on the poisonous drink called desertion - God still loves us and has made a way of escape for us beloved.

~It's not what you go through that defines you, but rather how you choose to respond to it that marks your place in history~

Romans 8:28 NIV says: *"And we know that in all things of God works for the good of those who love him, who have been called according to his purpose."* Yes, you may be faced with the obstacle of childhood trauma and learning how to forgive and move forward with your life in a healthy manner - but doing so will ultimately work together for God's good. You must forgive in order to be better, not bitter. I declare that in Jesus' name! "Amen."

Being a parent is a challenging assignment. Being a great parent even the more. Parents are expected to have a sense of duty to love, lead, guide, discipline, nurture and direct the children God has entrusted to them. Some parents wish, but acknowledge that children were not born into this world with an instruction manual or a down-loadable app that would teach how to keep their baby happy and successful.

Parents have been gifted with amazing insight to shape and mold the minds of their children. They can either bless or curse their children with their words, actions or the lack thereof. The Lord has placed an extraordinary amount of love in the hearts of the parents towards their children.

When a child doesn't feel a connection or acceptance from a parent, there is a breech in the love line somewhere. You may have heard people say that they have never felt love from their parents. Realistically, a person can only give what they possess. Being a part of a sexual act that creates another human being doesn't mean that the person possesses what's needed to love, nurture and direct that child.

We especially find this in teenage pregnancy. Once the baby is created, the parents don't know what to do with the life that has just been given to them as a result of their actions. So the teenage parent is left feeling cheated out of life and ill-equipped. If the parent doesn't have a genuine tank of love and affection for themselves and others, how in the world can they be expected to help raise a well-rounded individual?

When these things are not in place or have been abandoned, the children are left to care for themselves. Instinct and survival modes are the only means for a lot of children that have been given a distorted vision of what real love, leading, guiding and correction entails. The children must learn how to survive on their own - at times physically, emotionally and financially.

It's really remarkable how we don't have to be taught how to survive. Our instincts will kick in and get us through. If the parent does not prioritize the things that are a part of a healthy growth environment, then the children are left with distorted images of what parenting should or ought to be. The child will very quickly look to the street for what they should have been receiving at home.

No matter what anyone says, being loved, guided, disciplined and directed are not - I repeat, are not curse words. If a child doesn't receive the adequate training at home, their new parents are called 'Mr. and Mrs. Survival' and instinct will teach them to only think of themselves. Survival will instruct them to disregard another's feelings and property - where proper instruction at home would have taught them how to be kind, considerate and thoughtful of one's self and others.

One of the dangers of survival and instinct teaching our children instead of physical parents, are there often times isn't a date for course completion. If the child doesn't stumble onto Christ or is directed to Him, he will be encouraged to sign up for extended courses.

How the child struggled to survive has now turned into a normal way of life. "*Survival mode*" desires to be a part of our children's lives forever. Scrounging to survive, living pillar to posts and not having a steady job or housing are some clues that you are still in survival mode, even right now in your life.

Survival would love for us to become good friends with his pal's spirits called 'vagabond and bastard'. Vagabond would love for you to keep wandering around never finding peace in stability, while the bastard spirit wants you to keep feeling the emptiness of being abandoned. The bastard spirit will keep you feeling empty, even when the word of God tells us that whatever state we find ourselves in to be content.

My parents were young when I was conceived and as a result, there was a lack of knowledge concerning child-rearing. They had 2 girls born out of this union and I believe in the beginning, they thought they loved and would care for each other. I just don't believe they knew *how* to love and care for one another. We all have our quirks and we all have differences that make us who we really are. I know for a fact my father's different views on how things should and ought to be done -

versus my mother's views on how 'life is a party, don't take it too serious attitude' did not make for great ingredients in the pot of stew being served for family dinner. The result was a meal that was chock-full of a lot of hurtful actions and words.

We often heard, "your father is this and your mother is that." And such a whirlwind of words exchanged. Parental behavior should be that of respect and maturity towards each other. Parents should be the examples of what is right in the world. Their behavior should be such that their children would want to mirror their own lives after them.

Children often will duplicate exactly what they see in their homes. So for the sake of the world getting a taste of what you as a parent are cooking, choose your mixture of ingredients carefully. This recipe will live on from generation to generation, just like grandmom's homemade sweet potato pie.

Finally after years of neglect, disrespect, emotional and physical abuse, my parents parted ways. However, there was still a prize to be won. The children - my sister and I, now became the golden calves in their heated divorce proceedings.

Each parent was only concerned about themselves, never really noticing for a moment how it was affecting their children. It's funny how many times parents will fight, risk going to jail, curse and fuss at all who pose as a threat to their children - but they cannot see when they too are the very ones who pose the biggest threat. My sister and I endured many challenges imposed upon us through our parent's actions, decisions and words. What's even sadder is that there were plenty of adults who saw our dysfunctional family and they simply turned a blind eye. A child left to care for itself has no other choice but...**TO FIGHT!**

A child living and growing in a dysfunctional family has no choice but to FIGHT. Fighting is the only way the child feels that they can be heard, get attention or to just get everyone to be quiet until the next round. A child's FIGHT mindset at times is not to win the FIGHT, but to gain some of the power that has been snatched from them. They are being seen as only a child.

Children are people too and have real feelings just like adults. If you are in a dysfunctional life style and your babies are witnessing what's going on, stop it NOW for their sakes. Stop introducing your children to worlds that they should not have any knowledge of. Your conversations, poor behavior and actions are speaking volumes to your child. They too will lead a path of duplicating what you have shown them and will think it is acceptable, right or wrong.

We as parents take the liberty to discipline our children when they are doing wrong. The discipline is supposed to be a time-out in order to think about your actions and is supposed to correct the negative behavior. Well some of these parents need to be placed in time-out for causing harm and probably provoking everlasting physical, mental and emotional damage to their children. If those particular parents continue on that type of path, the Department of Corrections will fill these vacancies very quickly.

The purpose of this book is for you to do self-examination of your own life in many areas and to repent, correct and adjust accordingly. If you choose not to take heed - those children that have watched and encountered the childhood abuse, will ultimately be the ones who will be the decision-makers in your senior life. Senior-citizen homes are over-populated with seniors whose families have just dropped them off at the door and sped off, never to return again. No phone call, no visits, no pictures. Much of this is as a result of a non-existing or a total loss of a parent/ child love connection.

The lack of a love connection can make it very easy to simply deposit the senior onto another's lap to be cared for. If we don't self-correct our parenting, many of us will be left alone to die. I don't know about you, but I definitely want to be a part of the lives of my children, their children and my great-grandchildren.

Senior homes are sometimes the warm revenge the children were seeking, just to get even with their parents. Parents, I implore you to sow well into your children's lives that you may reap well in your later years. If you choose to sow the evil - well, let's just say a happy trail will not be your lot.

God's word is true, *"Whatsoever a man sows that ALSO shall he reap."*

I had to learn and learn quickly that it was ok to FIGHT back in the midst of my parents' erratic behaviors and dysfunctional mind-sets. If I hadn't, I promise you I don't know where in the Sam Hill I would be. Because my parents could not get themselves together - more times than not, my sister and I dealt with family members who could have cared less about us, or our feelings. My parents' actions resulted in a little girl - *me*, to console them once they realized they had gone too far again. I learned first-hand how God will always make a way of escape for you.

Before the divorce was final, my parents tried the shared-custody option. I just told you how destructive they both were and it doesn't take a rocket scientist to tell you this too was not going to work either. It was my father's weekend and my mother had to drive us to where he lived. My mother was clearly over him, but he kept a short-handled, every-ready battery-operated torch for her. My mom didn't tell us where we were going for the weekend. She knew if we found out prior to going, that there would be some trouble from my sister and me.

My father's side of the family lived a lifestyle that was quite the opposite of my sister and me. This side of the family was loud, argumentative, rude and very selfish. They didn't care what they said or how they said it, nor did they care how you felt about it. They were very strict. My mom knew that we would have cried our eyes out had we prior knowledge of where she was taking us. Even though she didn't verbally say where we were going, her driving route told me immediately.

My mom was a creature of habit. Just about every place we visited on a regular basis had its own driving route. This warm summer day was no different. I lowered my head and asked why we were going over to this side of the family's house? I asked if she knew that they didn't like my sister and I (mainly me, because I never accepted their sadistic humor of picking on me). She said she knew we hated it, but he was our father and that's where he is. She then reassured me that it was only for two days and she would be back on Sunday to get us for school on Monday.

We finally arrived at our destination and my father came outside to get my sister and me out of the vehicle. I did my best to stay in the back seat of the car hoping no one would notice that I hadn't gotten out of it. My sister had made it safely onto the pavement and carefully placed her thumb back into her mouth while waiting for me to join her. My father walked to the driver's side of the vehicle. There he and my mother had some type of intimate verbal exchange. What started out as a private conversation, turned into a very public display of aggression.

He wanted her to turn the car off and to come in and she wanted to just drop us off and to keep going. My mother was not buying whatever my father was trying to sell her. My father being the textbook definition of a stubborn man, reached into the car to turn it off as he had asked her to do several times.

My mother started to scream and curse at him. The passenger rear door where I sat was still opened when my mother put the gear in drive and proceeded to speed off. She dragged my father down the street for half of a block. While his torso was in the vehicle and his bottom half was kicking around on the outside of the door, is when I was spotted in the back seat. Dang Poppa! I thought.

I know it's sad, but what I was seeing didn't bother me in the least. I had become numb to their behavior. It was more devastating to me that I had been spotted, because I was still hoping that I did not have to spend the weekend with this side of the family. He yelled that I was in the back seat and that was the only reason my mother stopped the vehicle. I was in the back seat getting happier the longer her foot stayed on the gas pedal. Every second equated to me not having to go back to a place that made me want to throw up every time I thought of it.

Finally the car stopped and my mother told me to get out and go with my father. With my head held down I slowly got out of the car, said good bye to her and looked at my father - I was very upset that he couldn't hold on a little longer. I

REALLY did not want to stay with this side of my family. My father brushed his knees and motioned which direction he and I would start to walk. I told myself this wasn't going to be that bad, because it's only til Sunday. Because the earlier exchange with my parents was now turning into a long-weekend argument, as a result - my Monday never arrived.

My father would not give us back to my mother. My sister and I ended up staying there a little over a year with rarely a visit and scarce phone calls from my mom. When my mom would call, someone was always listening in and telling me what I could or could not say. We had to start in a new school. There were times when my mom would sneak to see me at my new school. These were the best surprises, but filled with the most anxiety because she would have to leave.

There came a time at my father's house when I wasn't allowed to ask when I was going home, where my mother was or even if I could call her. My aunts thought this was rather hilarious. They would often try to speak in code to one another and say 'MC called today to speak to J and C'. This always made me want to rip their eyeballs out.

My paternal grandmother had a nickname for all of her eight children. This particular aunt's name was 'bald-headed winch'. I had to be about 10 years old before I realized that this was not her given name. This family could call you out of your name on a regular basis, but you better never try it. Every time

I heard this aunt speaking her code, which really wasn't a code - I would say in a way not to be heard, *"that's why you are a bald-headed winch,"* and then roll my eyes like my life depended on it.

I really couldn't understand why my mom couldn't just come and get us out of this God-forsaken place. It had gotten so bad, that my father had said real randomly on a summer day that his new girlfriend was our new mom and to never ask about our birth mother again. I never really could understand why he wanted to keep my sister and me so badly; it wasn't as if he ever spent any real time with us. We were simply in the same household. Could he have only wanted my sister and I because he knew that was the only way to make my mother hurt as bad as he was hurting?

A day or two later I had all I could stand and couldn't stand anymore - yes sir, I felt like Popeye. I decided that if my mother wouldn't come for us then we would go to her. I thought maybe she thought we didn't want to be with her. I made up my mind that I was going back to my mother. I was sick and tired of being spoken to any old kind of way. Kids have feelings too. I processed it in my mind how to make the great escape with my little sister, who was till sucking her thumb.

Every FIGHT doesn't require fists to be thrown - sometimes you just need to run like the wind. I was going to run like my life depended on it, because to me it really did. My only question was how fast could my sister run? I knew that I could out-run the warden, (*my aunt*) who was given charge to watch us for a few hours. I was determined to get to my mother's house as fast as I could.

Since my mother was a creature of habit, I knew she would arrive and depart the same way. I knew exactly what route to take. I was even prepared to punch and bite the warden if she got close enough or tried to stop me.

So on this warm day, we were outside sitting on the steps. Not allowed to play, just to sit. Not allowed to talk, just sit. *I told you it was bondage.* The warden went in the house to answer the phone. I grabbed my sister's hand and asked if she wanted to go see our mommy. She nodded her head in affirmation. I said *"I need you to run as fast as you can and I will get you some popcorn"*, it was her favorite. I yanked her free arm and started to run - her other hand was connected to her head because she was still sucking her thumb. We made it to the end of the block without being detected. I was waiting on the light to change for our safe passage to the other side, when I heard my name being yelled. Aw man! 'It was the warden!!

I yelled to my sister to move faster, we must go quickly and she chose to move at a snail's pace. By the time I got us across the street, I noticed the warden was gaining on us. I had a choice - to either leave my sister who could care less where she stayed, or to give up and surrender in order to make sure they would not be mean to her. For the sake of my sister I gave in and had to suffer the consequences for my actions. Yes, that meant being beaten by the warden. I promise you I would have made it to my destination if I was alone.

In a FIGHT you have to think about the innocent bystanders and casualties. As much as she worked my nerves, the only one I gave permission to be mean to my sister, was me. While slowly walking back realizing how close I was to freedom, I said to myself, *if I was by myself that bald-headed winch wouldn't have been able to catch me*. I knew I had to think of another plan to get away. I would really have to consider whether I would take my sister with me or come back, break in the house and get her at a later date.

During that same summer we were outside, still just sitting watching other kids play. The phone rang, I was told to go get it and it was my mother. I was so excited, but I didn't want anyone outside to know it was her. I was so happy to hear her voice that I froze right where I stood - tears streaming down my face, when all of a sudden I heard my father come in the house behind me. He asked who was on the phone. I couldn't bring myself to say who it was and he yelled, "*Who is it on the phone?*" Instincts kicked in to say my mom, but due to my father's prior instruction, my lips said, "*THAT lady*". He stood over me and said "*What did I tell you to say to her if you spoke to her again*?"

With my heart beating at a rapid pace - my eyes full of tears and my mind trying to figure how to speak in code to let her know that I didn't mean what I was about to say, "*I don't want to talk to you anymore and I don't love you anymore and don't call here again!...*" Is what came out of my mouth, followed by CLICK.

My father was so proud of me that he brought ice cream for everyone. Again I could feel the FIGHT in me raging and preparing for another battle. *I must get us out of this place.*

The summer was just about to a close. I had just come from the store for my paternal grandmother. My hair was unkempt: I had on a t-shirt and a pair of cut-off jeans that I was now wearing as shorts. I had on a pair of sneakers that I had proudly decorated the laces with dangling metal circles from can sodas.

Everyone in my grandmother's house generally stayed in her bedroom since it was the only room where air conditioning was being used. The grandchildren learned to accept the daytime soap operas, as if the reality of our lives wasn't dramatic enough. The doorbell rang. The warden ran down stairs and answered it. She came back upstairs and told my grandmother that it was MC. So immediately my ears perked up.

I'm thinking, if she's here then she knows that I didn't mean what I said to her - or is she here to beat me because she had in fact believed that I felt the way I'd said? Either way I really didn't care. I just wanted to be with my mother. My grandmother then says *"Julia and Chrissy go downstairs and see your mother"*. I slowly grabbed my sister's free arm because the other was being used to occupy her mouth with the thumb-sucking. I didn't want to run, scream and holler because I knew that if the warden thought I was enjoying seeing my mother, we would be held back. We slowly walked down the stairs to see my mother's beautiful face. With our arms outstretched to hug her she gave a very quick hug and said "*Go get in the car we are going home.*" Some kind of way cement had filled my worn, metal-circle-top sneakers. I couldn't move. I heard what she'd said and believed it too. However the beating I had received for trying to run like Kunta Kente, was still fresh in my head and on my behind. I told her we couldn't go because my sister only had on a t-shirt and panties and I was going to get into trouble with my father.

My mother grabbed my face and said *"you are not spending another moment in this house, now get in the car"*. She picked up my sister and right outside she had a car waiting with another female passenger inside who waited to close the car door behind me. My mom had a brand new car that was bright and shiny. Blue outside, white leather interior and even with the windows down, it smelled fresh inside. She threw us inside and sped off, quite like that day with my father. I was so happy, but so afraid all at the same time.

The front door was left wide open and the smell of burnt rubber filled the street. I was certain we were going back to my maternal grandmother's house. However we never made it there. My mother had known she was coming to get us for a while. She took us to a female friend's house. When we got inside, there was a room prepared for us with brand new clothes, jewelry and shoes. My mom gave us a bath and did our hair. *Oh how I missed my mom pulling my hair up into a ponytail, then twisting the ends and adding barrettes!* She cooked us a meal and we just watched TV. I was so happy that the apartment wasn't that large, because I didn't want my mother to be out of my sight for one moment. We stayed there a few days.

As much as I loved being with mommy every night, I was filled with terror. I really believed my father would find us and scale the apartment wall to get inside. I knew if he got into the apartment he was going to beat us all within an inch of our lives. Thank God that never happened. Slowly we were able to piece our lives back together again.

From time to time my parents would argue. If they argued Monday afternoon - then like clockwork Tuesday afternoon during recess, my father would come and steal us out of the school playground or he would lie in wait for us to get out of school to snatch us up while walking home.

My father never wanted my mom to be with any other man except himself. He would go through great lengths to prove to her how he was not prepared to leave her life. One time she was visiting family in Georgia. He wanted her to come back to PA. When she refused, he went to go get her. I remember him getting all dressed up, picking his afro saying he was going to go get my momma and then we were going to be a family.

How many of you know that you can't make a person do something they do not wish to do? You and I know that, but somehow my father never quite understood that concept. He went to GA. I don't know how long he was gone, but when he came back he had a black eye and a bruised ego. He said to me, *"Look at me this is what your mother did to me. I just wanted to bring her home to you girls and she had men beat me up".* Could you imagine what this must have done to my psyche as a child? Seeing my father beat up and hearing my mother was involved. I felt I had to take sides, but whose?

Both parents had shown that they were not very stable. I didn't know whose side to choose, so for the time being I stayed neutral. This time I chose not to FIGHT to get to the truth. I chose to stand down. A person can only FIGHT when they feel they have a reason or right to defend themselves, or on another's behalf. I didn't have either.

There was another time that my parents argued, cursed and fussed. Again my father could not understand that my mother had in fact moved on with her life. The only connection between them was my sister and I. Well, my father found out my mom had a boyfriend. During the argument, my father had asked for my sister and me to come outside because he wanted to see us. My mother resisted for a while, but finally gave in. She told us to come outside and see our father. Reluctantly we complied. Before we knew it, he grabbed both of us and threw us into his awaiting car. All of the kicking, screaming and pounding on the door could not get it to open. He sped off just as my mother had in years prior. The only difference was that my mom was not hanging from the car. She stood in place numb, perhaps thinking it was a cruel joke and he in fact was only going around the block just to prove some weird point. I remember looking back, barely able to see her face through my tears. I thought, he is going to kill us for sure now.

My father was seething mad. He was cursing about her and calling her all kinds of names. Then he got a revelation to confront the man that my mother was currently dating. He wanted to win my mom back. How many of you know that even if my mom would have stayed with my father, her heart had long been disconnected from his. When a person has moved on in their lives, desperation will try to convince the one who is still embracing the torch for them, that the 'last hurrah' has not taken place yet. Don't try to hold on to someone that has long gone, let it go.

~ Don't try to hold on to someone that has long gone, let them go~

My father in essence wanted her badly; it didn't matter that she did not want him back. Beloved - that's not love, that's not the kind of relationship you would want your children to mirror in their own lives. We drove until he calmed himself down. We swung by my paternal grandmother's house for him to go get something. When he got back into the car he looked at how scared my sister and I were. He broke down and cried. He said that he just wanted to be a family and to give us the best he could. Even though I had a controlled hate in my heart for this man, even though I thought he was in fact going to kill me by sundown, even though I knew in my heart this man was pure evil - all I could manage to say was "*Don't worry.*" I told him don't look back, to look ahead and do what's right. He turned and looked at me, amazed that this 11-year old child was comforting him in his time of need. He said *"You are right,"* then he said, *"help me find where your mother's boyfriend lives, I have some business with him."* I told him I didn't know where he lived. I told him to ask her.

Fear suddenly gripped me again and I felt all choked up. So the tormenting car ride begins again. After driving all over the city trying to find this man's house, my father grew even more frustrated. He became so irate, that he began asking me if this was the man's residential block and if I gave wrong information, he would slap me. This happened several times. He hit me because I couldn't find where my mother's boyfriend lived. He never hit my sister or even asked her anything. Once he hit me, he told me I better not cry.

I remember staring out the window talking to a God whom I hoped was listening: I was trying to make eye signals with the other drivers that would stop at traffic lights with us, all to no avail. I was thinking this man is a ticking time bomb and if I don't give him what he wants I will not see tomorrow. Can you imagine the fear that kept rising inside of me? Can you imagine the feelings of helplessness I felt while preparing for my next slap? I genuinely had no clue where this man lived. He never stopped to feed us or to take bathroom breaks. He must have realized I was trying to signal a police officer because he abruptly moved my head from the window and told me to look straight. He huffed and puffed and threated to tear down all that was near and dear to me.

Finally, I believed that the God in whom I was praying to must have heard me. For I mustered enough strength to say in order for me to get there you got to go back to my mom's neighborhood. He did just that, but had warned that if that didn't work there was going to be war. He took me back to the neighborhood and the door locks were broke. I had every intention of jumping out of the car with my thumb-sucking sister. The only choice I had was to try and direct him to my mom's boyfriend's house.

This turned out to be very successful for me. I was able to get us to the house. He left my sister and I in the vehicle for which seemed like an eternity on a Sunday night. Once back in the car he said *"Thanks."* While driving, I had the relief knowing we were on our way back to my mom's.

You can imagine my surprise when he proudly told us that we will never see our mother again. We went to stay with him for the next two to three weeks. We stayed at hotels and motels every night. We had to wash out our clothes in the bathroom, eat fast food and stay in the car during the day while he worked. He repaired copying machines for various businesses. He didn't have a desk job. This type of job kept him in the field all day long. All my sister and I had between the both of us was her doll baby, a coloring book and the car radio... most of the times. We had to stay on the floor as he instructed, he didn't want anyone to know we were in the car.

I didn't have a desire to run because I didn't have a clue where we were. He really didn't seem to care that we were not in school, or away from our mother. Again, he didn't spend quality time with us - he only had possession of us. Finally I had my fill of him and I wanted my mother. I was tired of not knowing what was going on, or where we were. For the most part, we stayed on the same strip of hotels every night and I was very familiar with my evening surroundings. I had to wear the same pink corduroy pants, day in and day out. I was so tired of seeing those pants. I said to myself, *we are going home.*

So I came up with a plan. If you fail to plan, then you plan to fail. The next night the routine was the same. He would get us a hotel room and then go across the wide highway to the fast-food place called Roy Rogers to get us something to eat. The highway was so busy, it would take a while to get across it and back again. My father took our dinner order and said he would be right back. I watched from the hotel room window to make sure he crossed the highway. When I saw him entering the restaurant, I told my sister to keep watching TV. I picked up the phone and dialed zero. I said *"I want my mommy can you get her to come get us*"? The kind operator had to make sure it wasn't a prank. I told the lady to hold on because I had to make sure my father wasn't coming back, because I would get into trouble by being on the phone - now the operator started to take my call seriously. She asked my name and other information. I told her I only knew my grandmother's phone number, SH8-8366. I told her my father had taken my sister and I from my mom and we have been in hotels and eating nasty fast food. I put her on hold again to check.

Now I started to get scared because I couldn't see him anymore. Then I saw he was making his way out of the restaurant. She asked what was near me and I told her the names of what I saw, including my father's name. I told her I had to go because he was coming back for us. I asked that she please hurry and get my mom and then I hung up. I ran and sat near my sister as if nothing ever happened. As long as she was able to watch cartoons, she never moved. Maybe she knew that she needed to get her eyes full of the cartoons, because tomorrow we would be back in the car all day. We ate dinner and he was instructing us to get ready for bed, when there was a loud bang at the door.

A male voice was asking for the door to be opened. He hesitantly opened the door, police lights were everywhere. People came out of their rooms trying to see what was going on. My sister and I were escorted to an awaiting police car, while my father went to another vehicle in hand-cuffs. It was a long night, but none of that mattered when I saw my mom's face again. My maternal grandmother was so proud of me for remembering her home phone number that she never changed it. That number just got cut off about 5 years ago, only because she moved to Ga. The next time I saw my father was in court, where I had to explain all that took place.

Bullies like to slap, punch and throw people around - especially those that cannot or will not defend themselves. I was tired of being bullied by my father. I was tired of feeling like it was my fault that everything was going the way that it was going. I was tired of handling big-girl issues while I was still a little girl. These issues were never mine to handle. I had one too-many slaps. I too, chose to FIGHT. I had to fight to get my normal life back. I never laid one hand on my father but I called the ones who could, the Police. I didn't have to swing, jab or throw a body-blow, but the authorities did. They got my sister and I away from him and gave my mother complete custody of us. The custody battle was long and hard but in the end, no one could ever take us away again from my mom.

It's never too late to FIGHT for your kids. They need you and no one else can be a better parent to them other than you. Stop letting people, your situations and circumstances dictate your rights with your children. Don't allow past failures to keep you from your current victories in the lives of your children. If you don't fight for them, who will?

~Round 3~

O Baby

Loss of a baby

"Come to me, all you who are weary and burdened, and I will give you rest. Matt.11:28 NIV

The birth of a baby is usually a joyous occasion, no matter what the circumstances surrounding it. Just as a birth is a momentous milestone in one's life, so is that of a death. The death of anyone can be a very traumatic experience.

I had not realized depression had set in me. I had not recognized what being a functional-depressed person really looked like, until I happened to pass by the mirror one day. It was just an ordinary random day, or so I thought. This particular day it was rather sunny out with a mild temperature, no rain, nor a cloud in sight.

All was going well, just like any typical day of any given week. Got up - check, kids fed and ready for school - check, hubby off to his day – check. The last stop was for me to make it to work and start my day off as a teacher's assistant for a group of amazing, talented and funny 7th and 8th graders who only required emotional support while they were being specially-educated. While driving to work I loved to sing and listen to music. Did you know that your car can help you multi-task in so many areas of your life? On this day, my car became my recording studio. I truly believed my singing was top-notch, but I'm sure it was more like hollering. It would have made anyone run to get plugs for their ears.

On this particular day I was singing a song called the "Prayer of Jabez" by Donald Lawrence. I was convinced that I sounded better than the soloist herself. The music was turned up loud and I was singing my heart out to the Lord, as if screaming to the top of my lungs would make Him hear me better or more clearly. As I reached the part ..."*keep your hands upon me that no evil cannot harm me*"...I heard the Lord ask me if I was ready to hear the answer to a question I had once asked Him. His voice did not shock me, as I had mastered and had become quite familiar with hearing His voice at this point in my Christian walk. Whether He spoke softly or forcefully, whether He spoke through situations or people - I knew it was without a doubt my Father who was requesting my attention.

I abruptly stopped singing my solo, closed up my music recording studio and pulled right into a gas station lot that just so happened to be placed very conveniently on my right-hand side. I don't really know why I went into the gas station that just happened to be in the right position for safety, at the right time. I have heard the Lord speak to me before, but this time I was a bit puzzled. I realized that I had physically stopped what I was doing in order to give the Holy Spirit my undivided attention - something I have never had to do before. Other times when I've heard the Holy Spirit speak; I was able to continue whatever I was doing during His conversations. However this particular time was a little different. It was almost as if I didn't have control of the vehicle I was driving. I truly believe the angels that were on duty that particular day went to God on my behalf to ask if they could gently guide me off the road, as they knew He was about to drop a bomb-shell of a revelation on to me.

I assure you, at this moment I didn't have a care in the world. I didn't even care about getting to work on time. I turned the vehicle off and waited patiently again to hear from my Father. Again He said, *"Are you ready to hear the answer to your questions?"* Now, I talked to God on a regular basis and was always asking questions, making comments and trying to figure things out. I didn't have a clue as to what question He was referring too. I resolved that any question He chose to answer would perfectly be ok with me. I just assumed my question storage bank was getting full and He wanted to create space in it because He knew I had more to come.

Then I heard the Lord Say, "***Remember you asked me why I didn't let you have your most recent baby***?" I gulped and realized that this question wasn't on my list of top-ten questions. I slowly replied, "*Yes.*" I then heard His answer: "***The wages of sin is death, but my gift is eternal life***". He reminded me of a few years ago when I was pregnant with my 3rd child and the fact that I had not trusted him. I did not believe He would provide for me.

The Lord then said, "***You didn't trust that I would make it work out for your good. You really did not believe that I was there for you and thought I did not understand your heart. I am God, your God and I will always know what's in your heart. Because you failed to trust me and my Word, you terminated your pregnancy never once consulting with me. You used your own liberty and killed what I created. You chose to end what was to have life and life more abundantly. Yes, you felt guilt and shame, but was it because you knew I didn't approve of your actions or was it due to the fact that you felt you couldn't hold your head up after exercising selfish reasoning***"? Then fast forward to now: "***You again are pregnant with your 5th child and almost lost your life. I spared your life. Because you felt that you are in a better place in your life you believe that you are now ready for another baby. I did not allow this to be so; I needed you to understand what it means to be spirit-led. I needed you to understand how important it is to seek my face and hear my voice in the most challenging of times. I know all of the reasons that you convinced yourself that an abortion was permissible. None of those reasons affected me because they***

were not sent by me. I gave you a gift; you spit in my face and gave it back. I did not allow you to die. However, I could not reward good for the evil that was done. Yes, I have forgiven you and you will be better from here. You are now to encourage others in similar situations to trust me like never before. You are stronger than you know and you will recover." He then told me: ***"Wipe your face from those humbling tears."*** As I started to get myself together, He said: ***"Oh and one more thing, the reason I did not answer this question when you asked about a year and a half ago, was because you were not mentally ready for the answer. I never ever wanted to kill you. Now dry your face and don't worry about work. I have not allowed you to be late today. I have instructed you through my word to obey the laws of the land as well as mine."***

I regained my composure and reached my job successfully: His words were faithful and I was not late. Not only did I arrive to work safely, but also had a couple of moments to spare. When the Lord spoke to me, it felt as though a lifetime had gone by, yet it was only a matter of minutes. Thank you Lord.

I'm sure you may think, "Wow," this sounds harsh from God. However, it's quite the contrary. He tells you in His word that He will chasten those whom He loves. He saw the best in me even when my life was in shambles. He knew I would do just as He had said and He knew that my awe (*fear*) and love for Him would cause me to never revert to my own selfish ways. This was remarkable and momentous for me. I had begun to understand a lot as this conversation rolled on. I walked around in a funk prior to this event, never really knowing why or even when or if it would end. Singing songs didn't help as it would in most cases, to help rid me of negative feelings.

When the Lord finished speaking, it was as if a weight of about 5 years was lifted off of my shoulders. I truly needed to be forgiven by the only one who had the power to do so. I truly needed a cleansing like only the Lord could give. I needed to know that I was alright with him.

My sons Owen III and Julian are 11 months apart. For 2 weeks they are the same age. They are part of what makes a genuine smile come upon my face each and every day. I didn't really understand what being in love meant until I held Owen III and, I didn't know that I could possibly have an additional storage tank for another, until I held Julian. My boys have been such an inspiration and have motivated me to be a better parent and person, they deserve that much. I was still dating my-then boyfriend Owen and was not sure if he and I would make our relationship long-term. I am very happy to report he is now my wonderful and amazing husband...

I can honestly say that I never dreamed of being married, let alone having a fairytale wedding. I could never imagine living a grand life with a white picket fence, 2.5 kids and a dog. I had always thought one day I would get married, but it was not on my top-ten lists of things to do. Now I did think when the time came, I hoped it would be my current boyfriend/baby daddy asking me to be his forever. I did not live my life trying to reel him in or nag him about it. I TRULY just went with the flow of our relationship. I was happy living with him and very ecstatic that we had just had out first baby, Owen E. Ford III. He and his father, Owen E. Ford, Sr. were so excited to have their name continued in the family. When I first started to date my husband, there were no grandsons in his family.

On a nice summer day, I sat on the front porch with my boyfriend and his parents. I was about 16 or 17 years old. I REALLY do not remember how the conversation began, but I remember boldly declaring to his parents that I was going to give birth to their first grandson. They all snapped their heads towards me, then looked at my boyfriend as if to ask if he needed to tell them something. We laughed for a brief moment, then - as if in disbelief, I was asked to repeat myself. I said to them again, "*When the time is right, I was going to have your first grandson to carry on the family name.*"

I did not know much about the Prophetic Ministry then, but it has come to pass. What I prophetically-declared has come forth into existence. My sons are now ages 19 and 20 years old. Recently, they discovered a family truth. If neither of them had sons, then the FORD FAMILY NAME would cease to live on. My sons jokingly call themselves the alpha and omega, the beginning and the ending of the FORD FAMILY NAME.

They are well aware of the importance of having sons to carry on their family's name. A month after the birth of our first son, my boyfriend asked me to marry him. It was definitely a surprise. He was holding our baby boy downstairs in our living room, waiting for me to finish getting dressed for an event we had to attend. I walked downstairs on October 31st, a Saturday that was so sunny and bright. I had to shield my eyes as I finally entered into our living room where he waited.

My son was such a happy baby, he sat proudly on his Daddy's lap, flinging his hands all around almost as if he knew what his Daddy was about to do. My son had my engagement ring on his finger. It was so huge on his tiny little fingers and it almost could have fit as a bracelet. I saw a sparkle coming from the baby's hand and couldn't imagine how my one-month old son was able to get hold of glitter. As I approached even closer, I saw a ring. I looked at my boyfriend, his eyes were very soft and warm and his face was wrapped with a beautiful smile: he said "*Will you marry us*?" I did not think that I could love him any more than I already did. This day my heart expanded. A year and a half went by, then the birth of our 2nd baby boy, Julian Deon. We were finally lawfully-wedded husband and wife, Saturday March 19th, 1994.

I didn't like a lot of the examples my family had set on how to raise a family. I didn't want a lot of kids whose only means to survive would be through the department of welfare. I also didn't want to have kids and raise them alone as a single parent - and I didn't want to have my future children in an environment where fights and cussing was the normal way of life. I didn't know much, but I knew for a fact that this type of life style I would not duplicate.

Having those examples in memory - coupled with not having anyone willing to talk with me and help sort things out, is what led to my decision for an abortion. I honestly thought I was doing the right thing. I thought that I would be okay with my decision. Little did I know there would be a cost to every decision I made, whether it was physical or spiritual. I did not understand the amount of shame and guilt I would feel. I thought I was tough enough to handle the pain.

I really wasn't prepared to handle such a heavy weight alone. Even though my boyfriend was right there with me through it all and was prepared to accept whatever decision I had made, I still felt as though I was all alone because of the additional baggage in my life at the time. I had not completely given my boyfriend access to my heart. It wasn't until the birth of my first son that I truly understood what receiving true love meant. By the birth of my second son, I finally accepted what true love wanted to give me. Yet, I still gave limited access of my heart to my boyfriend. My boyfriend demonstrated and expressed his love for me in many ways, but my heart was impenetrable during that period in my life. Often times his words and acts of love were muffled by my state of mind, which prevented me from receiving it as I should have.

I had not cleared my spirit of this wrongful deed, the abortion. I had only masked it. Then after a while I carefully placed these emotions in my invisible book and placed it on the shelf in the library of my heart. Many of you know that no matter how sturdy a shelf may be, it can and will fall down if too much weight is applied. Inevitably, the time of falling down and crumbling came a few years later, right after the birth of my daughter, Milan.

Even in the midst of your disobedience and rebellion, God will always give you what you need, even when you don't realize it's a need. That's how I explain the birth of my only daughter. I never asked for a daughter, I was perfectly content being the only woman in my home. Milan turned out to be the breath of air I needed in a dry, humid place in my life. Milan was our unexpected surprise. Just when I thought I couldn't possibly love another as much as I loved my sons, here she comes. When the Lord blessed us with her I felt a sense of relief and believed I had done something right.

Child-bearing was filled with many challenges for me. Each pregnancy was filled with pre-eclampsia, diabetes, toxemia, etc. The doctor advised prior to the birth of Milan that he didn't think it was wise for me to try and have another child following her. He said that either I and/or the child could lose our lives. Well, I don't know about you but I was never one for playing with death. The spirit of Death and I really have nothing in common. After advisement of possible death, I clearly and quickly agreed to the tubal-ligation procedure. Upon you signing the agreement, the fine print says that there is a 1-percent chance that you could still get pregnant. Trust me - the hospital isn't looking to give you a glimmer of hope in reaping the rewards from a lawsuit. Instead they make sure you can't sue them for malpractice in the event you do get pregnant.

Milan was all of 3 years old, full of life and curiosity. My boys were adjusting to their new school while hubby and I were blissfully-happy. Then the record stopped abruptly with the news that I was pregnant again with our 5th child. I now became the 1%. We were all excited, re-assigning room space and discussing household changes, playing with possible names while trying to guess who was going to spoil this baby the most. Eight weeks into the pregnancy, the doctor's exam showed signs of the egg residing in my fallopian tube, but not to worry because it happens often and most times the egg will float right back out of the tube. So now we were in a 'wait and see' mode.

I'm a licensed cosmetologist. During this time, I styled hair full-time. As a precaution, I cancelled every client's hair appointment for a week. All I could do was pray. I felt as if my prayers weren't being heard. I felt like they were coming out of my mouth - shooting up high in the sky and falling right back down, just like the fireworks on the fourth of July that will explode with excitement, then quickly fizzle out.

It is week 12, time for another doctor's visit and I am sure that I will receive great news. I did not know this would be my final pre-natal visit to the doctors. The doctors looked at me sadly and said that the egg was still in the tube and it would not be possible to carry the baby to term. I just knew they had to be speaking to someone else in Japanese, because there was no possible way that they could have been speaking directly to me. Didn't they know I had given up a week to pray? Didn't they know we were making big plans to adjust to a new baby? There was absolutely no way they could have been speaking to me. But in fact they were. When I looked up, I guess I appeared to be in shock or in a daze to the nurse and doctors. The first words that I remember hearing was, *"Mrs. Ford, Mrs. Ford did you hear what we said? We have to make an appointment for your procedure, which day of next week is good for you?"*

Often times when one major thing in our lives goes south, it seems as if everything else is soon to follow. At the same time that my life was hanging in the balance about my baby - the landlord from whom I rented space for my hair salon was transpiring to evict me because he did not want to make necessary repairs to the salon. My vehicle was suddenly in desperate need of repair, as well as other things in my life. Things were falling down and breaking apart all around me.

The bookshelf that held all of my emotions, my pain and grief was about to collapse. Depression crept in through the cracks on the bookshelf built up in my heart. The bible says in *1 Cor. 5:6, Your glorying is not good. Know ye not that a little leaven leavens the whole lump?* Scripturally, Leaven represents sin. As a result of these series of unfortunate events, I had begun to entertain self-worthlessness, loneliness, anxiety, fear and depression. I was willingly setting the atmosphere for these emotions to come in and to make themselves right at home in my mind, heart and life.

Just hearing the news about not having the bundle of joy that I now believed I was ready for, sent me into a downward-spiral. I left the hospital still in a funk, not really sure where I was going. However, I am grateful that I wasn't driving - as I am sure I would have caused an accident or death. The Lord was so kind to me, even then to allow His precious Holy Spirit to lead and guide me all the way back home. You have to remember, this was the time before cell phones were main stream and the only communication I had with hubby was a pay phone. I had opted not to call hubby with this kind of news from a common pay phone. My heart kept telling me that this was not a common situation.

Once home, I had to figure out when to tell him and how to explain it to my kids. My marriage has always been founded on the truth and the whole truth no matter how challenging it may be to share. It's this type of truth that caused me to enter the house and blurt out we can't have our baby. The words just rolled off of my lips before I realized that I hadn't used much tact or even tried to brace him for what I needed to share.

The baby that I was carrying - the baby that we were extremely excited about having a part of our lives, was now not going to be with us. Of course, overwhelming guilt, shame and embarrassment filled my temple and mind. My mind kept saying, 'it's entirely my fault' and my heart was beating the rhythmic tune of 'it's definitely my fault'. I really believe that this was the moment when depression crept in.

I shared with him all that the doctors told me and then I kept telling him I'm sorry. That's exactly what shame and guilt will do to you. It will lead you on a path to travel with a heavy weight to carry. Every time you open your mouth you feel the need to apologize. I found that whenever my life situations would go south, whether I was involved or not - I would always be quick to apologize and try to right someone else's wrong.

My heart ached with the thought of having to tell my then 4-year old daughter and 8 and 9 year-old sons, that the family discussion we had a few days ago about our new baby would not be coming to pass. My lips felt drier than normal. I wondered since they were so young, would they even remember me telling them that I was pregnant. I couldn't figure out how to tell them, how much information to give or what to even to say. I am normally the kind of person who can find words to express myself at a moment's notice. Yet, I found this to be a most challenging task.

It had to be the Holy Spirit comforting me while my husband and I held hands and began to tell our children that their new brother or sister would not be joining our family. This was a difficult task because I wasn't sure how they would mentally handle the news and I definitely did not want them to blame God or hate Him if I told them He was the one who took their possible new sibling away. I also did not want them to get the wrong idea of where babies came from and where they go if the mommy does not give birth. The only thing we could think to say to them was the fact that our new baby was unable to grow and survive in Mommy's stomach.

There was a deafening silence after we informed them, they looked at each other and started to cry. They knew somehow that the news equated to death. They knew death wasn't a good thing. They knew it was a permanent situation which could not be undone. After all, they were made aware of this thing called death by way of the loss of pet birds and a crawfish they had previously had. My boys began to sob and Milan just joined in because she didn't want to be left out. I am almost certain she didn't really understand the true meaning of what was being said. She just knew that the mood in the room was very melancholy.

I believe that is what made her shed a few tears, because in the next breath she asked for ice cream. I am actually kind of glad she diverted our attention toward a more pleasant direction - ice cream. I had such an intense feeling of guilt and experienced irrational thinking so much, that I convinced myself that my children were going to need psychiatric counseling and very soon. One depressing moment can magnify and make every other situation join the depressing movement. If I was not careful, these emotions could take over and win! People of God, we must watch what triggers our lives into downward spirals. There is a demonically-influenced spirit that desires to take us off our paths of destiny. We must seek the root that is causing us to spin out of control. Every time the downward spiral button is pushed, we dance to the enemy's tune. When the enemy comes in like a flood beloved, the Lord promised to raise the standards. What is this standard He has promised us? Well, It a way of escape. It's called a breakthrough, a sudden burst of advanced knowledge from your current line of resistance.

When was the last time you had an opportunity to escape from your uncommon situation, but you chose to stay there because it was a place of comfort, a place that was familiar? Spirits of darkness would like to make you believe that they are protecting you under their blanket. Beloved, demons don't play fair. They really don't mean you any good. Demons don't care about your emotions or health - nor do they want what's best for you. Simply put, don't make friends with any of them.

After the children were informed that I would be in the hospital for a few days, I had to begin the huge task of packing and prepping my home for my recovery process. I remember not being physically or emotionally ready for this surgery, no matter how hard I tried. After arriving at the hospital, we waited for the doctors to do what they do. This was the day when it became official - from a doctor's perspective, that I do in fact have a high threshold (tolerance) of pain. I can take high doses of pain to the body without complaint. I wasn't trying to act like super-woman; however the pain I was being told I should be feeling never happened. The pain from the induced-labor never transpired. Instead of acknowledging that there was something a little unusual about my body's tolerance for pain, I chose to find God. My psyche had convinced me of a reason as to why my body was not responding to the general consensus of what the doctors thought.

It must be God saying that I will be able to have this baby, Right? Oh how I desperately wished it were so. As I laid there on the bed, I started to reason over and over as to why I was going to have this baby in spite of it all. I realized that I had come through many challenges in life and my child would also have to share the tag of... *"I too have completed the camp called hard knocks."* I envisioned that one day we would be sitting around chit-chatting about how we were told one thing by the doctors and yet God allowed another thing to happen. Ha ha, who would laugh then?

So what I thought would be a future family conversation filled with outstanding testimonials, was completely shattered. The doctors entered the room to tell me they were going to surgically-remove the fetus. They said that even though my body was not responding in pain as they anticipated, I was still in great danger. My thought...*did he just call my baby a fetus?* Someone clearly did not make this doctor aware of the new revelation that this is the second miracle child. The first, being the conception and birth of Jesus Christ.

The Doctor didn't get it, this baby - my baby, was going to go down in history as the one baby that has defied all odds and lived to tell about it. Yes, I was certain my husband and I were on our way home to tell the other kids the great news. I started to get up asking my husband for my clothes and shoes. He had to be at work in a few hours, the kids had school - I had things to do and a short time in which to do them in. Let's go home! My mind-set had now turned into actions.

While in the process of dressing, the doctors came into my hospital room and again asked had I heard what they were saying to me. Of course I had doctor, *you said you can't wait to be invited to my baby's College graduation from Yale University*...I heard you loud and clear. The doctors then started to say how they really wanted me to reconsider their counsel and stay to have the surgery. These doctors must be out of their minds!

The God that I have just grown to love and know would not allow me to go through the agony and pain that doctors are trying to get me to agree too. This God that I have spent my entire life running from and now am finally running towards, would not want me to leave Him again just after we reconnected - not if He loves me the way that He says. Impossible! Doctors, as I thought to myself, *I choose to believe the report of the Lord.* I believe that His love for me will most certainly out-weigh the words in which you speak.

Now, I was more determined than ever to get off of this bed of affliction. I did have a slight nudging pain, but nothing that kept me from moving around. It probably just meant bed rest for the rest of my pregnancy. This will be a cake-walk. The doctors realized that I was choosing not to respond to them, so they thought. I had just given a lot of responses to them, but I had chosen to keep them to myself. They then started to make a plea with my husband to have me stay for the surgery. After listening to the doctors, my husband reconsidered our plans.

How could he side with these vipers, after all, they just wanted the insurance money and to test out their surgical skills, how could he side with these people who did not know us? These doctors did not have a clue that we are awesome parents and would be that for this child as well. Now I am thinking about my husband, *I knew you didn't want this baby, I knew you were lying. Wow really dude? You could have just told me how you felt at home. I thought we were in this together. Why are you agreeing with the enemy who wants to take my baby, our baby? Don't you see this baby needs us more than ever? Don't you see that God must truly trust us to take good care of our baby as He knew these people were going to try and kill him or her? God wanted us to stand strong and not give in. We must take God's child home and wait seven more months to see our baby's face.*

In actuality, my mouth never uttered any of these words, but my heart was in the process of finishing the firm foundation of laying brick and cement to surround itself from ever feeling this horrible again. During this time, I had avoided my husband's eyes, until finally he realized it too. He and I both knew that if we looked into each other's eyes, we would know the truth. This baby was not going to be a part of our family.

We would know that this baby we had already started to pick out names and room colors for, would not be allowed to grace our presence - at least not on this side of heaven. My husband finally says, *"Babe, the doctors are feeling very strongly against you leaving here. They want you to sign a release paper saying that it is against their better judgment."* Then he said, *"Babe let's just stay and have the surgery, my heart is screaming let's stay."* How is it, *"let US,"* when really, it's *ME*? It's my body.

Now it's me against all of you. But when my mouth finally opened, I said "*Ok, we can have the surgery.*"

~A high tolerance for pain can mean you have mastered the craft of hiding all that affects you~

Beloved, we can go through so much in life, which often times will leave us feeling numb to other's adversities that we may find ourselves in. A high tolerance for pain can mean you have mastered the craft of hiding all that affects you. I have now received my PHD in the art of masking my high tolerance for pain, heartaches and frustrations. I guess I owe these accomplishments to the many overwhelming journeys stemming from my childhood. Feelings of hopelessness, loneliness and despair will wrap itself around us like a warm blanket on a cool night; whispering the promises of how they will never leave us nor forsake us, rocking us in their arms to the soft tunes of how they are the only ones who will ever be there for you.

When you have a high threshold for pain in the physical sense, trust me - I am sure it's the same in the spirit. Pain is pain no matter how or where you slice it. Pain is a universal language that even the legally-deaf can hear clearly. When you have a high threshold for mental pain, you start to become defensive and you are easily-offended, you believe that there is a great conspiracy against you and whatever goals you are trying to achieve.

This high level of functioning pain has been a great teacher and has taught me how to still get the job done while FIGHTING through whatever is ailing me. These levels of pain will immune you to your true feelings. You will only focus on what is immediately in front of you. The ability to function through a high tolerance of pain will leave you void of your true emotions. This should not be. God desires that we feel and live victoriously. He wants us to know what love, kindness and acceptance feels and smells like.

A high level of pain will encourage you to take a swim in the river called DENIAL. A reality check will whisper, *"Your attention needs to be focused on the matters at hand,"* while the wide river of DENIAL is calling you in for a nice and long swim. Don't let the call to swim keep you from facing reality. The reality of it all is if you deal with what is actually happening around you at the particular time, you will actually feel much better and stronger. Somehow, we have been taught to run and shut down. Our Lord did not instruct this in His word for His children. He said to be strong and in the power of His might and to put on the whole armor of God. He even told us that when we are feeling weak, to declare we are strong and He will take care of the rest. In order to receive the things God has for us, we must be willing to put down the things the world has given us to play with. We cannot serve two masters. Either you will love the one and hate the other. Choose to serve, honor and listen to the master that truly has everything in His hands.

I awoke from surgery in a room that felt cold and drab. I felt like I was the only person in the hospital. I had to adjust my thoughts and remember why I was there. I immediately grabbed my stomach and hoped this was just a bad dream, but when I looked at my arm and saw the IV line I knew it wasn't, and I wept. For the first time in two months I was alone, no baby to talk to or make promises to. It was just me, the cold walls and a God I didn't want to talk to.

I cried for a while, as I fell in and out of sleep which was caused by pain medicines. Finally, the doctors and my husband came into the room. The doctor began to say how the partial hysterectomy was a success, but the staff had to move quickly to save my life. He stated that once I made the decision to have the surgery, they immediately took me into the O.R. Once inside the tube where the baby was located, they found that it had burst. He said the poison from inside of the tube had started to spread throughout my body.

The staff had to move quickly to contain it so that I would not die. The doctor said had I left the hospital, it was quite possible that I would have died en-route to home or shortly thereafter. He said no matter how fast my husband drove, he would not been able to save me, mainly because it is difficult to see the tube that was in question and emergency doctors would not have known the tube had burst. As he turned to walk away he reached back and grabbed my hand and said *"Someone was looking out for you."*

~Even in our ignorance God still loves us~

Beloved, even in our ignorance God still loves us. He is still sending angels to watch over us to ensure our safety. And in spite of myself, my attitude, my mindset - He still saw fit to let me live.

During this time my vision was very cloudy. I could not see much of anything because it was so dark. The sound of darkness can be so thick and deafening that it can muffle other surrounding sounds out. In darkness your senses are heightened for sudden movements. It will also make what should be comforting, harmonic sounds, echo brass and tinkling cymbals.

At the time due to my dull hearing, I couldn't receive what the doctor was trying to say. He wanted me to know that all is well and also tried to hint that the Lord had protected me without using His name due to his not being sure of my religious affiliation. Instead all I heard was my baby is gone and the God I had just come to know was now playing a cruel joke on me. I imagined Him in heaven having a great time with the angels at my expense. You and I both know that this wasn't true and would NEVER be true, but pain had temporarily silenced this knowledge. God doesn't set us up to fail. His word says all things work together for the good to them whom love Him and are called according to His purpose. We just have to be patient with how long that will take.

I wept again for days and nights, I did my best to stop while hubby and the kids were around. I didn't want them to ever think that they were not enough for me. I loved my children so much and dreamed of having a house full. Yet looking at my own I realized that I will never be able to have any more biological children and again I wept.

My husband and kids were very attentive to me and my needs. Not really knowing what to do, but were ready to do it at a moment's notice. I loved them even the more for that. At one time Milan wanted to read a book to me - she sat down with her legs folded and read very passionately from an upside down book. It was the best story of the wonderful world of *Blue's Clues* ever.

The pain of my loss didn't go away overnight. Watching baby commercials on TV made me sad as well as looking at calendars thinking of milestone dates and watching other parents with their infant children. While enduring this physical pain, the landlord of my business property was in the process of having me evicted - all while I had to recover my truck that had finally been repossessed. Yes, my world was extremely dark.

My heart was heavy and my mind was questionable at times. Even though I was feeling like this, I had enough sense to know not to place these heavy emotions onto my children. So if I could muster up enough strength to appear strong in front of them, I most certainly can FIGHT to get it together when they were not present.

A FIGHT is what it took to bring me out of that heavy place of depression. I had grown into mastering the art of appearing joyful to others while my insides were being ripped to shreds. I had to wake up every morning swinging at the demonic spirits that wanted to dress me in their finest apparel. Often times the afternoons and any moment of down-time were filled with a repeat from the morning. During the evenings, the enemy wanted to tuck me in bed with feelings of inadequacies and loneliness even while sleeping in bed with my husband.

The FIGHT deep down in me had to come from a place of not wanting to see my children mentally-disturbed and in need of counseling because I couldn't get it together. The FIGHT in me had to be continual - never quitting, never giving up. My husband and children needed and deserved for me to be in a better place and space. They depended on me.

How many people are depending on you coming out of your depression? How many people need you to come out of your funk so you can live a purposeful life with and among them? Beloved, I encourage you to find the FIGHT in you. Do it today! Do it now.

~Depression will have you focused on yourself and what could have been, so much so that you will never appreciate any current victories in your life.~

You must master coming out of depression. This spirit desires to take you away from your family and friends while you're still physically in their presence. Depression will have you focused on yourself and what could have been, so much so that you will never appreciate any current victories in your life.

Plant your feet, pull your right arm back and in an upper-cut forward motion, serve the enemy a punch right in his face. POW! Tell him he cannot have what belongs to you and your family any longer. The Bible says do not despise a thief for when he is found you can make him give you your stuff back 7 times. Pull your hair back, take off your jewelry, apply some Vaseline on and GO GET IT!

Go get what belongs to you. Your sanity, your happiness and peace of mind.

~Round 4~

Father Forgive Them

Church Hurt

Jesus said, "Father, forgive them, for they do not know what they are doing." Luke 23:34 NIV

Have you heard the saying, “Ain’t no hurt like a church hurt?” Unfortunately, but fortunately I have experienced this statement and found it to be true. When a person is out in the world doing worldly things, you expect the world to treat and respond to you according to the world’s system.

The world’s system is run by the angel of light, the god of this world, Satan. While being a part of his system, you can expect to have bumps and bruises, scrapes and blisters from learning a lesson the hard way and re-occurring tests. You can expect the enemy’s punishment to be harsh for trying to break rank and file. After all, he is the enemy. There is a cost to be free, beloved.

The enemy cares more about controlling your mindset. For wherever your mind will go, your body will have to follow. The enemy is always after that which he can never physically have, your thoughts and your mindset. Since he can't physically hold your mind in his hand to control, he will instead send you subliminal messages as to how and why your life would be far better if you would be completely-submissive to his urges and suggestions. Sort of how those Coke-a-Cola commercials are designed to convince you of why you should buy their product.

The enemy is a hard task-master. He wants to constantly keep reminders in front of you of how his rule is going to be tough. The enemy will do his best to train his captives through tools of fear. If the spirit of fear is administered properly, he can leave the gates which leads towards freedom open and the slaves would even never venture out. He could even allow the prisoners to walk around without shackles, but they will walk as though they had shackles on. When he has done his job correctly, the spirit of fear will now be the gatekeeper for those in captivity.

To some, the fear of the unknown can be more dreadful than the harsh reality they are currently living. 2 Timothy 1:7 says, *"For God hath not given us the spirit of fear; but of power, and of love, and of a sound mind."* If the fear of freedom is gripping you, I am sure that you are having a challenging time loving people, including yourself and I am most certain that your mindset is all over the place. Are you feeling as if you are not in control?

The spirit of fear comes in many forms; paranoia, schizophrenia and bi-polar. These mental states can change positive mindsets. You could have been under the enemy's rule for so long that you forgot how to think and breathe on your own. Satan is also called the prince of darkness. All of those that enter his kingdom to serve, do so in intense darkness. The darkness in Satan's kingdom is so intense that it prevents people from seeing their own hands in front of them.

Light deprivation can do a number on your mind and body. A person who is light-deprived will assuredly have some adverse reaction to the light once they are exposed to it. The Lord doesn't believe in trickery. He doesn't want his children introduced to or misled by a false light or a cheap imitation of himself. John 8:36 NIV says, *"So if the Son sets you free, you will be free indeed."*

The genuine light of Jesus Christ entering your life is enough to set you free from bondage and to free you from your taskmaster, Satan. The enemy is subtle and cunning and will use all forms of trickery to win over his opponent. He desires that we reject anything that could associate us to a Godly lifestyle. The enemy wants as many that will follow to come into his camp and reside under his dictatorship. It's amazing to me that people have such a challenging time submitting to and following true leadership, whether from the home life, on the job or in ministry - but quickly surrender all to the enemy and his rule. We easily rebel against the things of God without conviction, but will embrace the authority of Satan and his kingdom workers.

Hurt is hurt no matter how you slice it, or no matter which day you do it on. But for me, the hurt that I have experienced has been mainly gender-based.

In 2001, while attending a conference in California, the Lord spoke to me. He told me "***to get up, there's something I need you to do***", and then He asked if I trusted Him. Right after this experience, the Lord started to use me tremendously in people's lives. He would set up divine appointments so I could minister one on one with people. On airplanes, in restaurants, supermarkets - it didn't matter where. I said, "Father use me how you see fit." My Father in heaven did just that. He knew He could trust me with the hearts of His people. He knew that my love and fear for Him would provoke me to get others to have the same kind of relationship with Him as I did. I counted it a privilege and an honor to have the Lord trust me with so much.

I really believe it was this trust that led the Lord to say that it was time for me to minister out in public. He said "***This is the season to preach my word without compromise.***" I told God that I was good where I was. He didn't need me to preach in public. I begged Him to let me just hang in the back. I was perfectly fine ministering one on one to men and women who were in need.

Those prayers were never entertained. The Lord had been preparing me on the backside of the mountain, quite like David. When the time approached, I was able to stand before my current Pastor and tell him 'how I slew a lion, tiger and a bear, O my'! I spoke to the Pastor just as the Lord had instructed. Many weapons formed but were unable to prosper. The enemy wanted me to keep quiet and never to speak of God. However God blocked that and the time was at hand.

Many had gone to the Pastor and said that the Lord called them to preach. However for whatever reason, it never came to pass. Many women had grown frustrated and angry with the Pastor in this regards. I didn't say or do anything that would compromise my character or that would bring reproach to my husband and family. Many women gossiped that I had to be doing something immoral with the Pastor, which is the reason that he agreed to ordain me.

In the households of faith we are quick to tear down another brother or sister's success. We are quick to use our mouths against what God is clearly doing in the lives of the people as He so chooses. The reason many get jealous and envious of others is not really because the person was favored, but is most times due to the fact that God did not consult us. We believe that God needs an approval board to set one up or to take down another. When in fact - truth be told, God doesn't need us to agree with any of His choices. He's God and can do whatever He chooses, whenever He chooses. It is really up to us to accept it or deny it. His will is going to be done regardless of our opinion. Many are called but few are chosen, so the Word of God says. Simply, the chosen ones are those who simply answered the call from the Lord.

Women are impulsive and emotional. Women of God, we need to be very sensitive to our emotions. We need to make sure we are not being led down the wrong paths. Wherever we get emotional - we have the power to take our husbands, kids and all that is connected to us. This can very well be a road to destruction. Our emotions should never get the best of us. We should never be led by how we *feel.* Make it a point to be spirit-led rather than flesh-led.

The Bible warns of the dangers of lust of the flesh, lust of the eyes and the pride of life. Don't envy or covet what doesn't belong to you. For to do so, says that your Father in heaven doesn't have enough to go around in order to bless His children. I assure you that our Father has more than we could ever need or want. He is truly ready to bless our socks off at a moment's notice.

We are spending too much time in another woman's garden, trying to tell them how to pull up their weeds instead of focusing on our own weed-infested garden. Spend the same amount of time tilling the land, pruning and watering your own gardens and I promise you that your garden will yield much fruit, season after season.

Jealousy and secret envy are not becoming traits in a woman of God that desires to please the Lord in all her ways. Don't you know that your Father in heaven has cattle on thousands of hills? Whatever you desire, know that you can go to God in prayer. Pray that His will be done in your life. The bible says to whom much is given, much is required. We often get excited about the given portion of that scripture but tend to forget there is a requirement. We don't know what a person had to go through to get what they have. If you want what they have, then you have got to go through what they went through and it is not always a bed of roses, it's a process.

Ask God for His will to be done in your life. This way you will not have any regrets about what you asked Him for. It's similar to wearing a pair of your big sister's shoes. You saw her come alive on the dance floor while wearing her favorite shoes. You have heard so many people compliment her on how amazing she looks in the shoes. It even seems like she was able to master every step to the newest line dance in those shoes. You see the shoes from afar and want them for yourself. You imagine how those shoes would look on your feet, even though they are not the style you typically wear. You beg to wear them but your sister refuses you, because the shoes are out of character for you. She even tries to get you to choose another pair that would be more suitable and is your style. But instead of heeding her message, your mind loads and locks on what you want.

Well, because of your persistence, big sister finally decides to let you wear the shoes. You have made sure everything coordinates perfectly with the shoes - your handbag, outfit, hair, nails and makeup. You step into the shoes and are a little shaky. You disregard it and make your way to the dance floor, determined to strut your stuff quite like your sister. However when the same music is played, you are unable to keep your balance. You are not able to glide across the floor effortlessly like you have seen your older sister do millions of times before. Instead you are slipping and leaning off balance with the appearance of a plane readying to land, all to avoid falling on your rear. Why did this happen? Those shoes were never meant for you. They belong to someone else and have been broken in by her. The anointing that rested upon your sister while in those shoes, made what she did on the dance floor look flawless.

~Desiring what was never supposed to be yours pulls you away from what God desires for you and your life~

The true anointing of God draws and it has incomparable beauty. Desiring what was never supposed to be yours pulls you away from what God desires for you and your life. Spend your time wisely. Seek out the good parts that have already been prepared for you. There will be no regrets or embarrassment. You won't be left feeling foolish. What God has for you spiritually, emotionally and physically cannot be given to someone else - it has been designed specifically for you.

Women of God, you are fearfully and wonderfully-made. You are uniquely made. Embrace being distinctively different instead of settling for a cheap imitation, or a horrible carbon copy of the original. Love the skin you are in. You will sleep better and have less stress if you do. Know that your Heavenly Father did not forget to give you gifts of beauty and talents before you left heaven.

Don't disrespect God by having a tantrum and throwing back what He has already blessed you with. Be appreciative with the measure of talents and skills He has entrusted you with. Love God even all the more because He believes so much in you. If you stop and take notice, I'm sure you will realize that you have more talents than you think. Find your passion in life and stop trying to stomp and crush others. Don't even think about labeling yourself a hater. Instead, become an *innovator.*

In the name of Jesus I declare that by the end of this book, you will become more motivated than ever to complete those projects that you once put off. You will be rejuvenated with just the thought of your future. You will see that behold, all things are new. Yes, even you can become new. In Jesus name Amen.

Before the Lord could release me fully into our own ministry, there was another assignment that I had to retake *(if you don't get the lesson that is being taught the first time, you may find yourself re-taking the entire class)*. It wasn't that I failed the class or even failed the test - the Lord told me that I'm simply a better test-taker. I received a C+, when in fact I should have received an A+. Back to the classroom to retake this test on how to master Love, even when it doesn't feel good.

There were some new classroom examples that I had to get a hold of in order to get out of this class once and for all. I thought I was okay in dealing with the cattiness of women. I thought I had mastered how to combat shady women. I really believed that I was successful at overcoming offences from women. Well Beloved, how many of you know when the Lord is calling you higher; the higher the level, the bigger the devils? When I got the revelation of this calling, I know for a fact that I heard Mahalia Jackson in the back ground singing, "Move on up a little higher move on up a little higher."

My thoughts: *Okay God what's going on with this group of women? I kept my head down, spoke when spoken too, stayed out of the way - was respectful even when women gave me their imaginations to kiss.* I heard nothing. The Lord told me to fast for 45 days. In those 45 days, the fire got seven times hotter. Women were not speaking; women were in cliques, women in leadership actually telling other women not to work with me or not do anything I had asked. Women speaking to me disrespectfully, all the while I had to keep a smile on my face and a heart of forgiveness. I worked with a group of snakes hissing and taking jabs at my body. All the while, doing what I'm asked by the leadership. I truly understood what Apostle Paul meant when he said that when he sought to do good - evil was always present. Every time I wanted to give the devil a reply, the Lord Himself would shut my mouth.

The Lord said "***Continue in my way, don't look to the left or right, know that your good will no longer be evil spoken of.***" Finally at the end of my fast, the relief that I had sought the Lord about came. Sometimes Beloved, when it's time to FIGHT the Lord will simply have you walk away. The song writer says, "You gotta know when to hold em', know when to fold em', know when to walk away and know when to run." This was a time of knowing when to walk away.

I wanted to make sure I heard God clearly and my husband confirmed it was time for us to move ahead and begin our own work. Yes, I had to endure many painful times. However, I now realize that I had to in order to be able to unconditionally-love the women the Lord has currently placed in my care and to teach them how to do it as well.

God is tired of the fake and phony "I love you" sister hugs and lingo. He desires truth in our inward parts. When I say I love you, it's backed by an action. When I show you I love you, it's confirmed by my words. Yes, love is truly an action word. When I release myself to love you, I am not able to take it back. These words have to perform the service I sent it out to do, which is to love that individual. Once I genuinely loved the women offenders that were in the camp, the flood gates opened and my release was granted.

Father forgive them for they know not what they were doing. For if they had they would of known not to put their mouths and actions against your anointed. God I thank you for covering me even in the midst of it all. Thank you for giving me another chance to take the test and to pass. Thank you for letting my FIGHT simply be in my legs which allowed me to walk away.

~Once I genuinely loved the women offenders that were in the camp, the flood gates opened and my release was granted~

~Round 5~

I Love him I Do!

Marriage

And now these three remain: faith, hope and love. But the greatest of these is love. 1Cor. 13:13 NIV

I had already told you about the image of a man I was in need of and searched for. I never believed it would be possible to find true love. Honestly I didn't believe I was deserving of it. I knew a lot of things, had seen and heard a lot of things, but I never really had a clear idea of what marriage would be like for me.

If I based what I knew of marriage by my family's history, I surmise that my marriage would have ended with a divorce or I'd have lots of children and never get married. What I didn't know was how to break the cycle of divorce and chaos that plagued my family. I didn't know what it would take to be in a successful relationship.

I didn't know what made men stay and take care of their families. I saw what didn't work for my family and I knew I didn't want that. I knew there had to be something better in store for me. Could I receive it? Would I run him away? Would he love me for who I am?

Overbrook High School 1989. I was in the 11th grade. I was the captain of the majorette squad. We practiced almost every day. My friends and I would often stop by the gym to watch the wrestling team. It seemed every time I went, a particular chocolate brother was always winning. At the time I didn't know much about this sport, but I knew that every time this young man went out on the wrestling mat, his hand was being raised as the victor within a matter of seconds.

His team always gave him support and encouragement, although I don't know why - he was never out on the mat long enough to even break a sweat. I loved the way the team entered the gym. When they came out and started their drills, it was rather intimidating. The overall team had an outstanding record. I always had a weakness for a chocolate man if he was tall and slim. My future husband was very handsome to me.

I had previously known some of his teammates and I asked them who he was. They introduced us immediately. We played cat and mouse for a while. Then finally we went on a date. We went to see a movie called, "Twins" starring Danny Davito and Arnold Schwarzenegger. I really don't have a clue what it was about because we spent the entire time kissing. He had a car and was a complete gentleman. He drove me home and bid me a fair adieu. I remember thinking I don't know much about him, but I sure would like to see how far this could go.

He treated me like a queen from day one. He spoiled me rotten. Whatever I wanted for the most part, he gave it to me. He never took advantage of me. He never disrespected me. He never allowed himself to be a push-over or a punk. He was very quiet around people he didn't know, yet with me we could talk for hours. To the outside world it seemed like he was so serious, yet with me he always had something funny to share.

We became great friends. He protected me from any unsightly elements. He made sure my heart was always protected. I will always love him for that. My high school sweetheart turned into my best friend, then my husband. It seemed he was already prepared to be a husband before I was ever ready to become a wife, or a good one at that.

I must admit - I again, have my very own super-hero, my husband. I told you earlier how his characteristics resembled those of my super-hero uncles. God had smiled upon me to bless me with someone that wouldn't run at the first sign of trouble from my past or parents. He somehow gave him wisdom at such a young age on how to coach me through a lot of the challenging situations I found myself in while my mother was addicted to drugs.

I knew for certain he would throw two fingers in the air and sing Reggae style, *"I'm leaving on the next train don't know when I would be back again."* Instead, when I needed him most he was there without judgment, even when he may not have had a solution...yet he was there. I will always love him for that. It's really an awful thing to see your girlfriend's mother on drugs. I would often ask if he thought that I would turn out like that as well and he would gently kiss my forehead and tell me that was never a part of my destiny. I never quite understood then what he was speaking of, but it makes a great deal of sense now - He was there through it all.

A young man whose parents were the Afro-American versions of June and Ward Cleaver and a young lady whose parents functioned best under the title 'Mr. and Mrs. Dysfunctional' - somehow were able to make it work. It's been working for the past 24 years. GO GOD!

It hasn't always been great, easy and breezy. I, just like everyone else, had not come with an instruction manual - but I did come with something that was more like a warning label stamped in big, bold red letters **RUN!** My husband helped to remove the labels and loved me to life.

How many of us are willing to go the extra miles needed in order to get the person we declare our love to. I am speaking of my husband, but that goes for families, children, neighbors, co-workers and even those whom you have declared your enemy. Often times when we say that we love or are in love with someone, it's mostly under certain conditions or specific parameters. Our love will only go a certain distance with specific limits attached to it. I'm so grateful God doesn't love us like that. I love the scripture in Mark 2:4-5 *"And when they could not come nigh unto him for the press, they uncovered the roof where he was: and when they had broken [it] up, they let down the bed wherein the sick of the palsy lay. When Jesus saw their faith, he said unto the sick of the palsy, Son, thy sins be forgiven thee. These friends had such a love for their brother who was not getting well."* Their love for him activated their faith which provoked them to get him to Jesus no matter what. Do we have people in our lives that would tear the roof off of a house in order to lower us down to Jesus where we would receive our healing?

I have always shared that I came into our relationship with plenty of luggage just like Eddie Murphy and Arsenio Hall in the movie, *"Coming to America."* It was the scene where they were coming through the airport with all of that amazing Louis Vuitton Luggage. Each large piece had another matching piece inside, just a tad smaller than the main one. I came to our relationship just like that. I had a ton of luggage and never found time or help to unpack.

Because of parental situations, I became used to staying packed for the next adventure which always seemed to be right around the corner. The mountains of dirty laundry that existed within the luggage made it too embarrassing at times to unpack in front of him. Before I came to the understanding as to how much baggage I actually carried around daily, I walked through my life hitting many people with my heavy bags as I tried to navigate this thing called life. I knocked some people completely out due to the weight of my bags.

Have you ever been near someone on public transportation and they had a lot of bags? They try to adjust themselves during every turn and stop along the route all while trying to keep their bags near to themselves in hopes of preventing someone else from getting harmed. Even in your most honest attempt to keep people from getting hurt, squished and pushed by your baggage - it usually happens anyway. Then the person feels obligated to run to your aid because they too realize it's way too much for you to handle on your own.

I met my husband at the tender age of 16. I had not yet learned how to control my baggage during the ride. What's even worst were the many times he bent down to help me get it together and I ignorantly retorted, "*I GOT IT.*" The sad part was that I had this beautiful outward display of luggage that I felt belonged only to me. Since it belonged to me, no one had a right to try to take it away, even if it was for my own good -

knowing good and well that if I truly had it all together, there would not be a need for him to offer assistance to me.

Pride will often cause us to fake it like we can make it. The enemy would love for us to cover up instead of accepting help from those who clearly could be of service to us in our times of trouble. There were plenty of times I rubbed healing salve on my hands because the weight of the bags made them sore, I tried to apply a soothing cream of worldly pleasures to soften the blows of hurt that my heart had received over time. This was all to no avail. The ungodly luggage had in fact become a part of me and my makeup, my DNA (DIRTY, NO USE OF ACCESSORIES), if you will. This luggage was never mine for the taking, yet somehow I ended up being left holding the bag.

The people who were the rightful owners never came back to claim what was theirs from the very beginning. They never cashed in their claim check, no announcement on the P.A. system of life asking if someone has seen their distinctively-beautiful, handcrafted six-piece luggage set OF DEPRESSION, HURT, and GUILT.

I learned how to affectively navigate through my relationship with my husband, all while holding on for dear life to this luggage. How many of you know that two's company and three's a true crowd? My husband realized I was starting to buckle under the weight of carrying this luggage, since he knows me all too well.

My mother was in her prime, abusing street and pharmaceutical drugs while scheming for her next hit: my father was never around and when he did come, he wanted to play the role of the great and exalted ruler featuring himself, starring himself and directed by him. If things were not centered around the 'oh great one' he would step off of the scene, which worked well for me.

My husband had taken on the now-vacant role of super-hero, minus the shotgun and handgun. As long as I stayed with him, my father would never become openly-confrontational. My paternal side of the family had caused some major issues when it was time for me to get married. I did not agree to, nor allowed the exalted ruler to walk me down the aisle. My father's family boycotted my wedding at the last moment.

Finally my husband said enough is enough. He started to intercept phone calls and could feel the negative attitudes my family was giving me. He put a stop to it all, not to some - but to it all. He banned them from our home. He realized that it was up to him to keep this now-toxic luggage out of our home and out of our lives.

He knew I was starting to buckle and didn't have the energy to FIGHT. At that point, the FIGHT shifted over into his boxing ring. My husband took the gloves off of my hands, put them on his and held down my position. Sometimes in a FIGHT we simply need a break, a pause and momentary halt so that we can continue on. My husband chose to stand in the gap and filter that which was trying to come into our home and tear us apart. How could my family issues tear us apart? He didn't have anything to do with what had been going on for years.

The longer I stayed in battle with family issues, we knew it would only be a matter of time before my mouth, mindset and behavior would adapt to that type of environment. If I continued on that path, I would have treated him the same way I treated everyone else. I would have distanced him from me emotionally and physically, which would have ended in a divorce. I was so grateful that in the development of our friendship early on, we shared our joys and fears. I believe it was because of this that he knew what I really wanted in and out of our relationship. No matter how I acted he knew the truth about me. He knew deep down inside what I wanted and what mattered most to me, which were him and our kids. He knew I really wanted to forget every harmful joker and their luggage I had willingly-accepted. Because of this knowledge, he never gave up on us, on me and where we could and would be one day.

Without realizing it, I was sabotaging my own relationship - one that I so desperately wanted to work. Remember, I didn't want a divorce but also did not know how to have and keep a successful marriage. This time the FIGHT was clearly in my husband's hands. I really wanted to give up on everyone, not commit suicide, but to just check-out completely and emotionally.

I was prepared to fortify the wall around my heart once again - the wall that I had allowed His love to tear down once before. I love God for putting a FIGHT in me, coupled with a determination to never quit. But this particular time I really needed someone much stronger than I. Sometimes love, true love will cause you to FIGHT for what is right and for what is deservingly yours.

The Bible says let the weak say that I am strong and to let the strong bare the infirmities of the weak. We were every bit of this scripture, which came to life right before our eyes. In fact, at this time in our lives we were just going to church - we were not saved for real, so we had no knowledge that these scriptures even existed. God, you are always making a way of escape for us. The bible says; "*that a brother loves at all times but a brother is born for adversity.*" Yes he's my husband, but when I needed another strong individual to stand in the gap for me while I was weak, he was there. He loved me through it all and proved why as my brother in Christ - he was born for adversity. Our Father in heaven does the same thing for us each and every day. Whenever we are in trouble His word tells us that He is a strong tower and all of those that run to Him will be safe.

Sometimes it's good to have a buddy system in place to help ward off the enemy's attacks against you and your life. I'm totally honored to have that in my BFF, my husband. Just like the song writer says; *"He saw the best in me when everyone else around could only see the worst in me."* I know he is speaking of the Lord, but I can also equate it to my husband and his valiant efforts to save his wife from herself and from her family.

When we got married I didn't really understand what I was coming into agreement with when I said my vows. These were commitments that I said to the Lord that I would do my best to honor. I wish there was a version to say that he would agree to leap tall buildings in a single bound in order to protect her from all harm. He might have thought twice about making that commitment then. But he actually accomplished this year after year. I'm so grateful to report that my excess-luggage-carrying days are about gone and no more chains are holding me. We have endured and overcome births, deaths, struggles and hurdles - even religious folk trying to pin us against each other. I'm happy to report that we are still happily standing through the many tests. Because we were able to create a base of friendship no matter what the world, family or church tried to throw our way - we were able to overcome it all.

We have learned never to take people's dreams and visions of what our marriage should be to heart. Most of them mean well, however we are not them and they are not us. What works for us just may not work for you. It's so funny that most people who break their necks to give us unsolicited marital advice either have never been married or have had one or more divorces. We choose to allow the Lord to be our guide. He and He alone will direct our paths as husband and wife. It's been working pretty well thus far and we intend to make sure it gets better from here.

I didn't know what this marriage stuff was all about or if we were going to succeed. I had too many things not making much sense to me prior to meeting my husband. Once I did understand, life started to make sense. His unconditional love and care for me has caused me to want to be a better person for God, for myself, for him and our kids. I loved him from the first moment we met and even more now and every moment in between. I'm so blessed to have a relationship, friendship and marriage in the same way as Christ is to the church. Though the weapons may form, they shall not prosper. God will always protect his bride from outside attacks and even the ones from within. Christ loves His bride.

~Round 6~

For the 9 Months She Carried Me

The Death of My Mother

"And provide for those who grieve in Zion--to bestow on them a crown of beauty instead of ashes, the oil of gladness instead of mourning, and a garment of praise instead of a spirit of despair." *Is.61:3 NIV*

"Listen baby your mom is dead, her body is on the floor. What funeral home do you what her to go to?" October 11, 2011 10:15am, my world changed suddenly and forever. Singing the Billy Ocean song, *"Suddenly life has new meaning to me there's beauty up above and things we never take notice of you wake up and suddenly you're in love."* This was a day I should have been prepared for, or should have expected.

We are all going to die eventually. We are all going to see the God that we serve face to face, in order to give an account of our lives. I guess I have always imagined her passing when she was much older and frail. Not at the age of 57 when she still had so much to live for. Not now when I was just starting to appreciate her. After all of the drug abuse it seemed she was finally trying to get herself together. The bible says that we know in part and prophesy in part - and my mother's sudden death was a part that the Lord had hidden from me. Could the Lord have kept it from me because He knew I would have begged for more time? How much time could ever be enough?

So many phone calls we shared when our favorite shows or movies came on, so many comical conversations about the latest and hottest families, friends, and celebrities. WOW and now, a year later. I can't even believe I'm writing a book, let alone dedicating a chapter in my book about the impact of her death. Already a year later and it still seems surreal. Already a year later and I'm still trying to breathe since that cool Tuesday morning phone call.

It was the Sunday of our 2nd year Church Anniversary. My mother would often call me in the evening to hear all about church service and what God was doing in our ministry. I told her all about our 2nd service with the guest speaker and their music ministry. She was so delighted to hear what God was doing. Then we talked about how she wanted to come into my jewelry business as a business partner. I had just sent her a catalog. She was super excited to see all of the bling. I had every intention this particular week of surprising her with a few pieces in the mail. The last part of our conversation ended like most calls. How's your sister? As far as I know, she's ok and she'd say, *"Julia can you promise me that you will take care of your sister? I know she doesn't want to be bothered with me right now but she will listen to you. Can you please make sure she is alright?"* *My reply is of course I will I have taken care of her my entire life why would I stop now?* Finally I told her I was beat from the weekend's activities and that I was tired. I told her I loved her and she said I love you too and we hung up. I did not speak with her on Monday, which was the following day. That wasn't unusual. Tuesday before I went to work I thought of her. I was going to wait until I got off to call and tell her I was going to send her some bling from my jewelry collection. However that opportunity never presented itself. Instead I received a call from a family member in Georgia.

She said that her mother received a disturbing phone call about my mother. My cousin asked me to give my mom a call and to check it out. She said that her mother was unable to understand what the caller was saying to her. I said thanks for calling, I will give my mom a call right now. I told my supervisor that something was going on with my mother in Georgia and that I needed to step away from the work phone to give her a call.

In my mind I just knew it was about the jewelry. I just knew that she was telling people about what she was getting ready to do and the people were a little hesitant based on her track record of being shady. I figured I would just speak to her sternly to let her know what she can and cannot do and how she would need to slow down because she's not even in the business yet. However that time never arrived.

I proceeded to call her phone, her current boyfriend answered; I was a little aggravated because he never answered her phone. I said hello can I speak to Maggie? (I had given my mom the nick name of Maggie since I was in 4th grade, with her permission of course) He started to yell into the phone saying, *"She's gone! She's gone! My Maddie is gone!"* So in my mind I thought she broke up with this man and she walked out and left her phone in the house with him. I would soon learn this was not the case. I asked sort of nonchalantly, *"Man, what in the world are you talking about, she's gone? Well where did she go I retorted? Back to Midway, GA where her family resided? What do you mean Maddie is gone? Can you just put my mother on the phone and stop playing around mister?"* Then he says to someone, *"You tell her, I can't do it."*

My thoughts are, what in the world is happening down there? A woman who was completely void of ever being the owner of emotions got onto the phone - she says, *"Yea baby your mom is dead, her body is on the floor, what funeral home you want her to go to?"* DEAD? ON THE FLOOR? FUNERAL HOME? HUH! SERIOUSLY? NO LIKE SERIOUSLY? I MUST BE GETTING PUNKED? WHERE ARE THE CAMERAS? THIS IS SO NOT POSSIBLE.

The woman is steady calling out to me. I could not give her a quick response because I needed a moment to process what she was saying while asking God if this was in fact true. It seemed as if an entire lifetime passed by before I could muster up enough strength on the inside of me to continue the conversation. I didn't cry, I didn't scream, I needed to investigate and quickly. I believe this skill was acquired from all of the homicide investigation shows I had watched all my life. This was my cable-bill money at work. I had just spoken to her on Sunday I had thought, how could she be dead? I have never been one who becomes untied in the midst of anguish, a crisis or extreme turmoil. I have been given an amazing ability to stay very cool while working through some toxic and stressful conditions.

So now I'm writing down names, badge numbers and social security numbers. I want to hear what took place at least 3 times - yes sir, you will explain it to me as many times as I need to hear it, because everything you are saying to me sounds like a murder. So I proceeded to tell the police to lock up the boyfriend and keep him into custody until I could sort this whole mess out. Don't forget -I was the lead detective on this case, unofficially. I hadn't met this boyfriend officially. I didn't know how much he loved and cared for her. I didn't know the dreams and goals they shared. All I know is this man murdered my mother and justice will be served.

Had we met prior, this mindset would have never entered my mind. Maggie had a great impact on him. She filled his world with joy and purpose. Part of me was stilling hoping she had just overdosed on pills or just had blacked out from some pharmaceutical drug. This too was not the case and I was very quickly settling into what I was just told moments ago, Now I am saying to myself, *hold it together, get yourself together don't break down, now right now.* The police are on the phone asking what to do with the body? WHAT TO DO WITH THE BODY? I could feel my emotions coming to surface. THAT'S MY MOTHER! I wanted to scream, that's the person that made me laugh and cry at times, THAT'S NOT A BODY OR JUST A BODY, SHE'S MY MOTHER! She's the person that infuriated me most with her abuse of drugs while she made me the best salmon cakes ever, THAT'S NOT SOME STANDARD RUN OF THE MILL GOVERNMENT-ISSUED BODY, THIS IS MY MOTHER! The one that through it all introduced me to and encouraged me to find and keep a relationship with God.

I often wondered if it would have been easier to have just let loose on the police officer on the phone, or to just speak as normal as possible to get to a resolution? I know laying the officer out right then and there sure would have felt better. But the spiritual side of me said he was just doing his job, he has to be detached from his emotions - so I kept my mouth closed.

I was the next of kin and the body could not be moved until I gave permission. So in that case run it all by me again, how is it that her body is on the floor...again? After I was certain everyone in the room had given me all I required for my thorough investigation, I instructed them to take the body to the county morgue until further instructions.

Still not allowing myself to feel or really even cry. I had to strategize how to break this to my family, especially my 93-year old grandmother. My family is so amazing. As soon as I called and shared what took place, everyone flew into action like superheroes. They wanted to make sure my family was taken care of, making sure my oldest son was getting picked up from college and then everyone shared the same sentiment - let's not tell Granny right away. We all felt that was best for her. No matter what challenges lay ahead for you personally, you must always be prepared to be more concerned about someone else before yourselves. Everyone knew that my 93-year old Granny was top priority.

We agreed to disconnect her phone, which limited her communication to only two family members who were left the heavy task of telling Grandmom the sad truth when they and they alone felt it was best. They were her primary caregivers and I trusted they knew best. When they finally told her, it was too heavy of a blow for her. She lost track of things for a month or so. She only remembered certain people and certain things. She had been very conscience-minded and coherent prior to that time.

It's amazing how your brain knows when too much is too much. It was as if her mind went into protective mode in order to prevent overloading. Quite like a computer when it is running and you step away for longer than five minutes, it would go into a sleep mode to preserve the battery life. Well it seemed like once my Grandmom received the news of her youngest baby - the child who had certainly had her share of struggles in life had passed on, her mind shut down: it would not allow her to take in anything additional or unnecessary.

She was only able to remember the good and the people who mattered. As much as we wanted to protect her mentally, we could only protect her physically. Realistically it was her mind and heart that we could not reach to protect her from possible self-destruction. God is so amazing to have gone the extra mile as to protect my grandmother from the added stress of losing her baby girl. Don't get me wrong, she knew and understood what went on. However, it seemed like the Lord blocked her from experiencing agonizing pain by having her mind shut down ever so gently, just for a few moments. It was as if He was preserving her energy and life as well.

I had the honor and privilege to minister the word of God on the behalf of my mother and family. I thank God I was given the chance to do so. In true Maggie form, one service wasn't enough. We had to give her a service in Georgia and Pa. I pray she would have been proud of me.

I never ever prepared myself for my Mother's death, especially her untimely death. In the midst of grieving, I had to be mindful of my husband and children whom were and are very compassionate and thoughtful. They made sure we were there for each other. They gave me my moments to shed tears or to just stop and remember my mother.

However I didn't want to take this for granted. I didn't want my house to be filled with sadness forever, I was never asked to curb my emotions or to limit my tears. The mother and wife in me wanted to keep my home balanced in all things. So instead of having public displays of breakdowns - I retreated to the bathrooms, my pillow at night and hid in my bedroom for a while. I chose to cry silent tears: this was not as easy as it reads. My hurt, loss and pain were very real. I felt and had known that I was being put into a dark place and space where if I fully gave in to grief, I knew it would take the Lord Himself to come get me.

As comforting as the enemy called depression tried to appear, I had to keep FIGHTING against his attempts of trying to get me to come over to his house for dinner and a movie. Depression was courting me long and hard. He was salivating at the mouth while wringing his hands. He said to fear, death and anxiety: you guys could never get her to give up with all of the other attacks you threw her way in life, however this attack right here, this pain right here - this loss right here will sho' nuff be just what we have been waiting for not to just knock her down, but to kill her for sure.

The enemy wanted me to be spiritually-dead. He doesn't want us to look to rise from the ashes of despair nor to ever find a way out. It would mean so much to the enemy and his camp to get you to fall away, to waste away in your sea of hurt, disappointment and worry. He would put a feather in his cap as a sign of victory in Satan's camp. You and I can never surrender - we can never wave our flag.

Throughout this first year I had to fake it until I was able to successfully make it. Kirk Franklin sang it best,

> *I smile, even though I hurt, see I smile, I know God is working so I smile, even though I've been here for a while I smile, smile. It's so hard to look up when you've been down. Sure would hate to see you give up now. You look so much better when you smile, so smile.*

Even through the hurt and pain, we must go on. The days that my heart was filled with extra weight and my mind was racked with past memories - these were the days when I had to learn how to smile a little wider and brighter.

For me, the best way to pull myself out of the downward spirals of agony was to find someone who needed a friend and then encourage them. I LOVE to help to people. I LOVE to help people find their smile. Coming out of depression or any state that is contrary to the Word is not achieved through your emotions, for the day will come when you will not feel like coming out of your area of bondage.

My prayers are that you understand my fight to stay sane. Just like recovering addicts have to make a conscious decision to stay clean and sober, we who are spiritual must do the same. For our own spiritual sobriety, we must go after it like our lives depend on it, because it does!

~Round 7~

Father, I want to LIVE!

Health Scare

Dear friend, I pray that you may enjoy good health and that all may go well with you, even as your soul is getting along well.
3John 1:2 NIV

It's funny how we live our lives eating, drinking and doing whatever we feel we are big and bad enough to do. Carp' Diem! *"I am seizing the day,"* is what we tell ourselves, never mind the consequences of our actions or neglect to our bodies. Our bodies dictate our limitations, while our minds work overtime in overruling them. We can become stubborn and set in our ways - so stubborn that our mindset starts to tell us that our bodies will not be the boss of us and our lives.

Listen beloved, I learned the hard way to give an ear to the conversation my body would like to have. When it speaks and tells you to slow down, take your medicines or even to go to the Doctors. It's peculiar how we always want the Lord to save us from people, situations and even ourselves. We beg and cry for Him to send us a life boat to get us out of our pain and misery. Yet when He sends us a way of escape, like a Christian Doctor or medicine that actually works - we won't take it because to us it's not in the form we were looking for it to come in.

I've heard it said that ignorance is bliss, but with many of my health scare issues, ignorance was putting it delicately: I was just plain old stupid. You never know what God will use to get your attention. If we choose not to heed His numerous warnings and disregard the signs telling us it's time to seek professional medical help, our portion may be a grave. Our bodies are wonderfully-made. God installed alarm systems throughout it to warn us when something inside us is about to be sick, is sick or failing. *(You know, like cramps and headaches around menstrual time).*

The Lord had continuously allowed me to narrowly-escape death on multiple occasions. Each time I would genuinely tell Him thank you. Then I would turn right around and be negligent of my body's warnings signals. As a result, high-blood pressure and diabetes are my current ailments. I can't say that I have battled with these diagnoses for years, because I haven't done one thing to prevent them until now. I just surrendered to it most of the times or simply ignored it the other times.

I have seen too many recent deaths. Mainly that of my own mother, whom had a plethora of health issues due to constant neglect and abuse to her body and it finally gave out. My previous health scares never had a real impact until I saw how suddenly my mother passed away. I had lived as if I was never going to die. I ate and drank all that I wanted, when I wanted it. I knew that one day death would come knocking on my door, however the passing of my mother made that day more of a reality and rather quickly.

The enemy loves to operate under the cloak of darkness. He loves to be left alone. I'd rather expose the spirits that are trying to get me to conform to their ways. I'd rather have my own public reveal of the enemy and his attacks so that I can get the help needed, versus having a private meltdown and crash where the enemy gets the glory. Since my mother's death, the spirits of fear, death and depression have been knocking up for me. They want me to let them come in so I can entertain them all. I refuse to answer the knock. I refuse to let them in or have their way. Fear keeps whispering in my ear, "*You know you will die the same way. You will not have a chance to say goodbye to your friends and family.*" Fear keeps trying to convince me that I might as well surrender all to the spirit of death since he's coming for me suddenly also. The spirit of death is around just provoking me to give up to fear.

Death just wants me to know that he's on the scene and is waiting for a time to come get me. Death keeps saying if you won't give in to fear or let me take you, then you might as well let depression rock you to sleep at night. In fact let depression wake you up, meet you for lunch and tuck you into bed every night. Depression is a great soother for you since you miss your mother so much. Let us take you to her.

The weapon may form but they shall not prosper. I know this may be strange reading to some, but not to me because I am actively FIGHTING the enemy on my behalf of you and the prevention of starting a generational curse. He will do his best to stop you and to make you quit God's team only to link up and join his team. There are in fact demonic spirits, working in cahoots with one another to create your demise. Don't forget - the enemy comes to steal, kill and destroy. He desires the latter, to annihilate you. He never wants you to return and create a sequel to the original nor try to come back for revenge upon him.

This current FIGHT is a spiritual one. I can't win against the wiles of the enemy by cursing, fussing or stomping him out of my life and ears. I have to fast, pray and be obedient unto the Lord. I cannot waiver in my position for God. I cannot allow the enemy to toy with my emotions. Stability in God is the key. I cannot be off-balanced while trying to FIGHT demonic spirits who do not FIGHT fair. Every now and again the spirit of memory-recall will try a re-visit. He wants me to keep replaying every detail that led up to my mother's death. He wants me so distracted with myself that I would not be able to be of assistance to the kingdom of God.

These spirits would just love for me to invite another of their buddies into my life called Pharmacia. This spirit is closely related to prescription drugs. This is where we get the word *pharmaceutical*. This spirit desires for you to become a pill-popper. That too I refuse to do. What specific pills would they like me to take? Prozac, *which is an anti-depressant.* The definition of Prozac is no imagination. The enemy wants me to be so full of depression that I reach out to take pills that will prevent me from having dreams and visions.

These demonic attacks are trying to come after the prophetic anointing on my life. Uh so sorry, they have the right one on the right day. POOF be gone! Be honest with yourself and take a moment to examine what type of spiritual attack you were under after the death of a close person. Many of us don't want to express ourselves on a good day, let alone on the days when we are being attacked. I refuse to allow the enemy to keep pecking away at me while pretending that ignoring him will make things better.

Beloved, I'm prepared for things to get worse because I will never wave a flag of defeat to the enemy. Just as I'm preparing for the worse the Lord reminded me that vengeance is His. In most of my spiritual battles, my FIGHT is not one where my fists are needed. The only requirement for this FIGHT is a surrendered heart and mind, a bowed head and a physical posture for prayer. This is so easy I don't even have to break a sweat or mess up my hair and nails.

The Bible says; Do not despise a thief for when he is found you can make him give you your things back 7 times more. Are you really able to spot the thief that has been on assignment since your love one's death? God will always make a way of escape, for you to come out of the heavy deep dark depression that has been resting on you like a warm blanket since your loved one's death. The real question is, will you do what is necessary to accept the way out that you have been given? Will you sit back on the sidelines of life wondering what could have been, had you only listened to the Lord when He offered you a way out? The Bible says that we should never, absolutely never allow ourselves, anything or anyone to separate you from the love of Christ. Are fear, depression and death trying to keep you separated from the Love of Christ - the genuine love He has for you as His child? The enemy only has as much power as you will give him.

Many of us are still grieving while trying to cope with the pain, the absence and instability caused by the loss of a loved one. Don't try to reason with the gatekeeper to depression. Get into the Word of God. The Bible says that God has not given you the spirit of fear, but has given you love, power and a sound mind. Fear plaguing you? LOVE someone even the more. Find extra people to love. The Bible says that perfect love casts out all fear. The word perfect means maturity. Then the word says God didn't give us fear but he gave us power. Do you know the word says that we shall be able to tread upon serpents and scorpions without being harmed? The word also says that for as many that have believed in him; to them he gave the power to become the sons of God. The word power in this text is Exousia. It means to have the power of authority and rights. Did you know you have been given the power and authority to cause demise to the camp of the demonic spirits seeking your demise? The Bible tells us that one can put a thousand into flight. That means we are supposed to have the enemy on the run, not the other way around. Then the word says that instead of fear, God has given us a sound mind. That means a double-minded man is unstable in all of his ways. We cannot entertain the spirits of 'wishy and washy'. The Bible says God would prefer that we are either hot or cold. He doesn't want us straddling the fence when it comes to Him. He wants us to make our calling and election confidently. He has already done the same for us. God doesn't - nor has He ever wavered in His love, time and commitment to us.

Fear has such a way of creating suspicion in our minds. Fear can make paranoia one of our babysitters. If these spirits are plaguing you while you seek healing from the loss of your loved one, stop entertaining them. They are not amusing. If you need spiritual help in detecting what spirits are troubling you, reach out to your spiritual leader or email me. I don't proclaim to know a lot, but what I do know I will use it as a blessing unto you. If I'm not certain, I promise to direct you to another that could be a blessing to you as well.

One of the most recent attempts to make me surrender to the enemy came just a few months back. I fell very ill. I had pneumonia, my sugar level was 400 and my pressure was 210 over 130. Yes, my body was getting ready to explode as a result of over-working itself. When it was time to go to the hospital, the enemy kept trying to plaque my mind with thoughts that I would not leave out of there alive. He tried to get me to believe that I was going to die at any moment. He did his best to paint a picture of the actual scenarios that would eventually lead to my being coded-blue and then expiring. He wanted me to sign off emotionally with which scene I liked. It didn't really matter to him, because the end result was death.

I must admit I did look at the different versions of my proposed upcoming death. However there was one thing that I just couldn't seem to wrap my mind around. I WASN'T READY TO DIE! There was a renewed thirst to live that was down on the inside of me. My mother's death had started to deplete me. Mentally I was exhausted with all of the 'should haves, would haves and could haves'. I was beginning to become so consumed with the after math of death, that my current life was about to slip right before my eyes.

In order for something to be done to you, you must first allow it either verbally or non-verbally. If you lie down and let the enemy dictate your expiration date, then guess what? That date will actually come to fruition. If you hold on, the enemy will make good on his threats if you allow it. I really was not being led to co-sign to his huffs and puffs. It seemed like for every reason he showed me that this was the end - the Holy Spirit showed me why I must live. Depression will keep telling you reasons why you should just give up and die. But the Holy Spirit will always beg to differ. The Lord never desires for us to take our own lives. He and He alone is the giver and taker of life. We were not born with a case of heavy depression and failure, or a great amount gloom to use when we were ready to call it quits. All we would need to do is write in the check-out date of our choice. Imagine how flooded heaven would be if everyone was given the responsibility of writing their own death date. Only to arrive in heaven and learn you left here too soon. Only to know that there was so much more for you to do and lives for you to positively affect.

Imagine the conversations people would have while waiting in line to see the Lord. *"What brought you to this check-out line? I got tired of my financial debt, or I always said that a woman/man would be the death of me, or I told my kids that since they take me for granted, one day they would come and look for me but I would be gone - yeah that will show em', or I was so sad about so many different things that I wanted to find a much happier place."*

Once you arrive in heaven - you stand in the long lines and you learn at check-in time that you are not allowed in to spend eternity with whom you claimed was your Father in heaven, because you took your own life. If God really is your Father then why would He want you to go against His word for your life? Suicide and the thought of it is nothing new to God. He understands what we feel and go through. That's why it was so challenging for Him to watch Jesus go through the process of the cross. Despair and apathy can cause people - yes, even people of God to consider suicide. Here are a few examples of suicide from the bible:

Saul was stressed out, unable to live up to certain expectations; he felt rejected and a failure; 1 Samuel 31:4

Saul's armored bearer was led by impulse to commit suicide. He wanted to die with his boss. (40% of teenage suicides are impulsive.) Samuel 31:5

Judas was depressed, felt trapped by materialism and guilt. weight of the betrayal had not been a cost he had counted up Matthew 27:3-5

Here's what the bible says about us taking our own lives:

God has a great plan for our lives. God has created us in His image (Genesis 1:26-27). He created us for a purpose. God has a specific plan in mind for everyone. For I know the plans I have for you, declares the LORD, plans to prosper you and not to harm you, plans to give you hope and a future (Jeremiah 29:11).

God's plan is for life, not death. The Bible teaches that both physical and spiritual deaths are a result of our sin and disobedience to God, but eternal life is a gift to those who receive it.

For the wages of sin is death, but the gift of God is eternal life in Christ Jesus our Lord (Romans 6:23).

Jesus taught that death and destruction are the works of "the thief" (Satan).He said, *The thief comes only to steal and destroy.* (John 10:10).

John 8:44 says that Satan is a "murderer" and the "father of lies." The feelings of despair that lead to suicide are caused by some of his lies.

Jesus wants us to have life. He said: The thief comes only to steal and kill and destroy; I have come that they may have life, and have it to the full (John 10:10).

Life belongs to God. It is never our place to take our own life or someone else's life.

Do you not know that your body is a temple of the Holy Spirit, who is in you, whom you have received from God? You are not your own, you were bought at a price. Therefore honor God with your body (1 Corinthians 6:19-20).

We wait in hope for the LORD; he is our help and our shield. In him our hearts rejoice, for we trust in his holy name. May your unfailing love rest upon us, O LORD, even as we put our hope in you. (Psalms 33:20-22).

Christ promises that He will give us rest from our problems.

~The solution to despair and hopelessness is not suicide, but faith in God~.

Come to me, all you who are weary and burdened, and I will give you rest. (Matthew 11:28).

While in the hospital I had a critical decision to make. Do I really want to live or am I willing to call it quits? I looked at my family and I CHOSE LIFE. I thought about all that I would miss if I died right now. I would miss my kid's weddings, my grand and great-grandchildren's births and accomplishments. I would miss going on a cruise with my husband. I would miss watching him swim with dolphins while I ate sautéed lobster.

These were not acceptable milestones to miss out on. I thought about how if I died right now, it's possible for my husband to still re-marry. I couldn't stand the thought of that nor of another woman calling herself mother to my kids - especially my daughter. Nope, I wasn't having it. My husband has done an outstanding job raising our sons. My daughter, my only baby girl from my loins - NO, I could not entrust her care to another woman. My family visited me daily and stayed as long as they could each day. My kids got into bed with me, took naps, went in the hallway to get ice water, the nurses were bringing them snacks often. I'm okay, so I thought. I figured since I was in the right place to get help and as long as I was being administered the proper medicine, I must be okay. Physically that was true.

I had now become a compliant patient. I willingly started to take my meds and became concerned about my soon-to-be-at-home dietary and medicine regiment. However one night my family went home from the hospital. They had given me kisses good night and told me how much they loved me. Immediately once they left I was saddened. I could feel tears welling up inside of me. I hurried my family along so I could have alone time with the Lord. I wanted to know where this sudden burst of melancholy stemmed from. I said Lord "Why am I so sad? Why does my heart feel like its breaking?" He told me that I was definitely on the right road to physical healing.

My mind was finally being made up to take my meds and change my diet. Then he said he didn't want me to get my physical health confused with my spiritual health. He said I should have never felt content with my children lying in the hospital bed with me. He said by doing so, added them to my bed of affliction and invited my kids to get to know all the spirits that were ailing me, instead of teaching them how to FIGHT against the wiles of the devil. He told me never to invite others to become a part of a place where I have not deemed for them to grow.

My bed of affliction was my bed and not that of my children. It was my lot due to my disobedience, not theirs. I should have taught them how not to allow disobedience to influence them, to have more of a say in their lives than the voice of God. God didn't want my children experiencing comfort in beds of affliction. He desires we have an abundant life. He wants each of us up, walking and moving into better places. What often times happens is the places that were only designed to house us temporarily, will then turn into a permanent residence. I didn't want my permanent resting spot to be that of a hospital bed. I was much more than a hospital bed and all that comes with it. I needed to show myself and my family what it looks like to rise again from the ashes of a poor healthy lifestyle. ***I HAD TO FIGHT FOR MY RIGHT TO BE HEALTHY AND VICTORIOUS.*** Prior to this great revelation the doctors didn't know when I was leaving the hospital. Once I got this revelation and understood what I was to be doing, the next morning the nurses said I was going home.

At the end of each round of a FIGHT there is a 10-second warning count. Then the bell will sound for that particular round to end. Once the round has ended the boxer returns to his corner and refreshes to go right back into the FIGHT. While in the corner there are a few key people working on the fighter to make sure he/she is well-equipped physically and mentally to go back and win the fight. There's a cut man to make sure all open cuts are covered and protected from bacteria and infection, there's the trainer to make sure what was taught behind the scenes is being utilized properly or he explains to the fighter how to counter the attacks that have been coming his way. There is also someone there to make sure the fighter is well-hydrated with fluids and lastly, every super hero needs their own theme music and hype man: this person's job is to keep the fighter convinced, even in the worst part of the fight, that they can overcome any challenges that their opponent may pose.

Well beloved, in life we are told through His word in, 1 Tim. 6:12; to *"FIGHT THE GOOD FIGHT."* In order to do this we as children of God, need help as well. In the many rounds of FIGHTS that we will have to GROW through, there will be times when we will hear the 10-second count bell ring and know that the enemy may try to roll out some kind of heavy combinations in order to knock us down.

Our job is to stay on the offence and not to let him get us on the ropes. We must make sure we are able to counter punch every combination he thinks will knock us out and keep us from coming back to start the next round. Once the bell has sounded and the current FIGHT in our lives has taken a break, we are able to go sit down for a moment. While we are sitting down catching our breath we must know that we are only there temporarily.

No real fighter has a long time to regroup while actively engaged in a fight. While in our neutral corner, we don't have time to dilly dally or make small talk. We don't have time for fussing and arguing with those who are in our corners to help, encourage and motivate us. We must stay focused on the job at hand. One thing's for certain - we must have confidence in those whom we are allowing to have our backs while we are in the corner.

In addition to having confidence in your corner, you can't be easily-offended. Your trainer is liable to say some heavy things to you while you are prepping to go back out: you have to know his/her heart is towards you. You must know without a doubt that if they are speaking to you in this manner, that it must be with a beneficial purpose in mind. Also, when your trainer is in your ear helping to strategize for the next round, there can't be anyone else speaking to you. Your attention must be completely on the trainer's words and/or actions to show you how to get the job done.

We need to make sure our corner people are seasoned individuals that have our best interest always on their minds and in their hearts. These people cannot have evil thoughts, greedy pockets or manipulative plans towards you. Believe it or not people will do their very best to connect to you when they see you moving and operating in a Godly anointing that they deem unique. They will consider this to be a very valuable tool they can utilize for their own selfish gain.

~Be very careful not to associate with bloodsuckers. Bloodsuckers come to drain the very life out of you~

Be very careful not to associate with bloodsuckers. Bloodsuckers come to drain the very life out of you. They want whatever you have acquired that resembles fame, monetary gain or favor. They want what you have prayed, fasted and sought the Lord for. They don't want to do what you did to get what you got: they are much happier eating off of your plate if you let them.

One thing a FIGHTER needs while training, is a healthy diet. Even those in spiritual FIGHTS need a healthy diet of prayer, fasting and seeking God's face while inclining your ear to His voice. Once properly and spiritually-nourished, you will have enough strength to fight off the spirit of the bloodsucker.

We know who we need in our corner if we were FIGHTING a physical battle. Who do we need in our corner during our spiritual battles? My suggestion would be the following: Let your trainer be the Holy Spirit for He will always lead and guide you, let the balm of Gilead be your healing lotion for any cuts and scrapes you may of endured, get your rehydration from the true and living water Jesus Christ who will make sure you never thirst again and let your hype men be every person that ever said they have your back and every person who has ever rooted for you to succeed. I promise that this will be a winning combination!

The hospital stay was my bell-sounding alarm. While there, I was able to gain the instructions from the Holy Spirit. He told me just what I needed to know so that I would not lose this battle. There were some things He spoke to me while lying there in my bed of affliction that could have been interpreted as kind of harsh to the natural man.

How many of you know that while in time of battle we don't always have time to be politically-correct or gracious, especially when your life is on the line. What does it matter about how your corner people speak to you if they are keeping you from harm's way or saving your life? I understood what the Lord told me, all that I needed to do to counter some of the blows the enemy had thrown my way. The Holy Spirit wanted to make sure I was in the best position to win this next round. I told him **"I got it!"**

I admit prior to this great revelation, I had fallen and needed help to get back up. The blow of the sudden death of my mother had knocked the wind right out of me. The Bible says that a righteous man may fall 7 times but he gets back up again. I really believe it's not the fall that hurts so much, but it's the getting back up. It takes a great deal of tenacity and courage to get back into the ring called life. But I wanted to and *needed* to get back in it again.

I must admit I was face down on the mat of heartache, pain and emptiness. While there I saw my life, the ups, downs and the bad hair days. It's funny how the constant pains and agony we carry birthday to birthday seem to go away with one great big upper cut to our jaw. This kind of hit is enough to take the wind right out of you and make you reconsider if you want to get up and continue on with your life, or just stay there laying down on the mat of depression with the demonic spirit of **Fear** working as the referee, counting you out.

This is where I found myself. When I finally started to come to myself, I heard the numbers 5, 6, 7 being said by the enemy. He sounded as if with each passing number he had increased joy because it appeared as if I wasn't going to be able to recover and get back into the fight. However God said, not so. When the Lord saw that I was entertaining the enemy's voice for too long - I heard His voice just as clear say **GET UP!** It was the number 7 when He said this..., biblically speaking, 7 is the number of completion.

The Lord said that He has finished the work so I can get up and finish my race. He said that everything that was ailing in me is now completed. He gave me the expiration date for these past and current troubles. I GOT UP AT THE COUNT OF 7. Just as I was able to get up and get back to FIGHT THE GOOD FIGHT, you too can achieve this goal.

Change isn't change until it's changed and until you become sick and tired of being sick and tired - your body will not be able to pull itself up off of the mat of depression. The enemy called defeat is counting on you not to get back up again. He is happiest with you being on the mat with feelings of being despondent and lethargic.

It was when I heard the number 7 that I realized I can't go out like this. I refused to allow my children to feel sorry for me and I refused to put my husband through emotional turmoil. It was in this place that I knew I WANTED TO LIVE! In order to live, I had to dig inside of myself and gather as much strength as possible to be able to FIGHT once again and this time I MUST WIN.

I must win, I need to win. This time instead of running from the devil, I chose to bring the FIGHT to him. Instead of allowing the enemy the constant opportunity of being the aggressor, I chose to reverse the course of the FIGHT. The Bible says that one can put a thousand to flight while two can put ten thousand to flight. When I got released from the hospital I chose to find and put my thousand to flight. It was time for them to leave.

The Bible says do not despise a thief for when he is found, you can make him give you back your things 7 times. Well beloved, the thief has been found. It's not my husband, children, mother, father, sister or my brother. It's not my former religious leaders or their spouses, it's not my childhood memories or family members, it's not even myself. The enemy that has taken a stance to come up in opposition against me is the same one that was thrown out, not asked nor escorted out - but **thrown out of heaven.**

The Bible says in Revelation 12:9 *The great Dragon—ancient Serpent, the one called Devil and Satan, the one who led the whole earth astray—thrown out, and all his Angels thrown out with him, thrown down to earth.* This is my REAL enemy and he doesn't even have skin. Since my last and final hospital stay I have chosen to live healthier; mentally, emotionally, financially, physically and spiritually. I am no longer offering myself to be spiritually-depleted by intentionally draining spirits that operate through people.

I have intentionally chosen to get back up and into the FIGHT at the count of 8. That's right beloved, NEW BEGINNINGS. How about you? Are you too ready to get back up in to the ring of life? You won't have any regrets. Nothing beats a blank, but a try. No more excuses. Take the limits off of your possibilities. You will never know what you can do until you try. Stop waiting for the world to tell you what they think is best for you.

The Bible says in Philippians 4:13 *"I can do all things through Christ which strengthens me."* I heard some amazing young song writers creatively pen this in a song, I CAN DO ALL THINGS, CAUSE BIG IS IN ME, JESUS IS IN ME!.

Beloved, let this same mind be in you which is also in Christ Jesus. Jesus always knew who He was, how much He meant to our Father in heaven and how much power and authority He really possessed. With that He never took advantage of anyone, nor did He allow himself to be taken advantage of. He never allowed demonic spirits to make Him into a punk believer of His Father in heaven. Jesus always knew the true identity of the greater one.

That is now what we have the task of knowing also, who really is the greater one on the inside of us? Once you know that Christ Jesus is the greater one not only on the inside of you - but the one whom you have completely surrendered to, you too will be able to shout **FATHER, I WANT TO LIVE!**

~Round 8~

New Beginnings

Singing I can see clearly now, the rain is gone,
I can see all obstacles in my way
Gone are the dark clouds that had me blind
It's gonna be a bright (bright), bright (bright)
Sun-Shiny day.

Ahh, the lost art of breathing. Lots of times due to sudden life changes, we can experience a momentary lapse of air. It's funny how one of the things we need most to survive, is one of the most things we take for granted. A fresh of breath air is very cleansing to our lungs. It helps to regulate us.

For me, it seemed I had totally forgotten how to breathe right after my Mother's death. Something so simple, yet it seemed very challenging for me to do. Instead of breathing I learned how to hold my breath for amazingly-long moments. I would imagine this is what swimmers endure. *I really only could imagine this because I can't swim a lick.* I never learned how to swim. I just couldn't seem to master holding my breath for long periods of time - ironic isn't it? What I couldn't seem to overcome underwater, I had become a pro at on land.

This is supposed to be my last chapter. However you can trust me that this is not the end of my story. There is a reason as to why I chose to have eight chapters in my book. Each chapter had its own story; its own voice, its own path to travel.

Spiritually-speaking, the number seven represents completion. That is why the last chapter was so very important to me. It represented the completion of many poorly-directed B-rated, short film clips of my life. I'm proud to announce that stuff is officially over!

From this point on I will no longer remember or look upon those times in my life as points of despair. I will only revisit them if it will cause another to heal in their own lives. There are at least seven chapters in my life that I can boldly declare the FIGHT IS OFFICIALLY OVER. HALLELUJAH!!

Now this is chapter eight and biblically-speaking, eight represents NEW BEGINNINGS. I'm looking forward to all that the Lord has declared to be a new beginning in my life. Mary, Mary sang it best, "*I've had enough heartache and enough headache I've had so many ups and downs don't know how much more I could take see I've decided that I've cried my last tear YESTERDAY."*

One of the only things I don't regret that I picked up along my travels of life is my absolute love for music. I promise you I have a song for just about every occasion!

Every time I needed an escape, it came through music and finding the humor in the most serious of situations. I didn't realize how much music was a part of the fabric of my life until the birthing of this book.

I really believe that music kept me from suicide, insanity, deep depression, unforgiveness and hate. I have always heard that music can calm the savage beast, well it must be true and because of the races, I have had to run I needed help to keep me on the correct course. The Bible says that laughter is good for our soul; it's a good medicine for our spirits. I may not always be able to get a belly laugh out of every situation however - I promise you I can manage to get a chuckle.

I have learned how not to take too many things too seriously. I think I get my humor from my mother. She could always find some kind of way to put a spin on the situation and make it a light one. *God, I really thank you for the strength to laugh even in the most challenging of times*. I thank God that none of my vices were drugs, alcohol or a life of crime.

However due to low or no self-esteem, I had areas of struggle that only involved me.

Ah, I'm hearing another book, so stay tuned. While reading this I want you to stop for a moment and think about what the Lord has used to keep you on the straight and narrow. What interest do you have that has helped to keep you focused? If you can't think of anything, create one or two. Go find your passion. Go do something that is healthy for your mind, body and spirit. Do something that you will not regret or have embarrassment about in the morning.

I knew I had a book to write. I knew one day it was going to happen. Well, it has come to pass. Even though I knew I had to write a book I never really felt that I had anything to say. I hope that makes sense. Although in my early childhood I was quiet and laid back (I know that seems hard to believe) but my adult years have proven to be on the contrary. I find that I seem to have something powerful to say and something to contribute to just about any conversation.

Words of encouragement, a prophetic insight or something quite like that. **Parturition**: *the act or process of giving birth.* I was long overdue to give birth to this baby right here, my first book, "The Fight of My Life". It felt like I had given birth - or so I would imagine, considering all of my children were birthed through C-sections. I imagine that if I had to actually have a baby by natural means, it would have to feel like this.

I had to endure stomach cramping, I had to get a focal point in order to push this baby successfully through the birth canal. The enemy wanted me to take something to numb the pain of labor and delivery: something like drugs or alcohol or depression - something that would just take the edge off of past memories, past emotions and mindsets.

The Holy spirit said "Not so." I was able to give birth like a big girl! If I would of taken something to just help me to get by, I would have missed one of the most important parts about giving birth: seeing your child's beautiful face for the first time. Naturally-speaking, the faces are yours. It's everyone that was so kind as to take the time to read my story. I'm so very grateful that you heard what I had to say. The Lord did tell me that what He has placed inside of me was well worth reading.

I have chosen to live for Christ. He is the only one who can sustain me and keep me from the psychiatric unit. I was tired of figuring it all out when he had already worked it out! Told you I have a song for everything. You may have found yourself somewhere in this book. My prayer is that you did.

I hope and pray through my transparency you too are able to embrace the healing, deliverance and peace that you need to survive. It's nothing like listening to people who have really been through some things and are still alive to tell about it. For one, it's very therapeutic to the story teller and two, it encourages the listener to be grateful for where the Lord has either brought them through or kept them from. What is your story? We have heard it said, girl if I wrote a book it would be a great novel-turned best seller. I challenge you to get out what is inside of you. Tag, you are it! I'm virtually tagging you in to tell your story. Singing, *"You can do it too, punch a nella punch a nella, you can do it too punch a nella in the shoe*!" Don't only see the sad, depressing and heartache while walking through these pages; embrace the hope that comes with it, the hope of knowing that if it had not been for the Lord on your side, where on earth would you be?

Allow inspiration to join you with your cup of coffee and bagel. Be inspired to tell your story the way that only you can tell it. Dare to be distinctively different in finding your literal voice. I believe in you and want you to fly high above the mountains of your circumstances.

Yes, "I do believe that you can fly, I really believe that you can touch the sky if you think about it every night and day then spread your wings and you can fly away." You will find that your words - not someone else's, will give you the proper momentum to soar like never before.

I didn't run to FIGHTING, it was kind of introduced to me through life circumstances. I chose as to whether I would allow myself to be punched, slapped or kicked by life and its system of operations. I chose to FIGHT back. I didn't really know what this meant. My first FIGHTS didn't have any form; I was doing what you would call the 'row boat'.

How many of you know that if you do something long enough, you will learn how to mature your craft? Instead of row-boating and hitting any and everything in sight - the grace and anointing on my life is now such that I am totally in control over which FIGHTS I take part in and which ones I will never be a part of.

I can even see a FIGHT far off now because the anointing from the Lord will sharpen your vision. I'm in a new place of healing. My heart has taken a licking. It amazes me how resilient our hearts really are; our hearts can take an attack and still keep beating. Our hearts can be taken for granted, mistreated, abused and offended, yet it will still keep ticking.

A FIGHTER'S heart must be even the stronger. FIGHTERS are athletes and their bodies are trained intentionally to take a beating, to give and receive pain. This includes the heart; it must be conditioned to adjust to the many different body movements and routine stresses. Athletes are trained to keep their eyes on the prize no matter how much they endure. I have brilliantly discovered how resilient and forgiving my heart is. I believe it is due to this fact that I have been able to still stand.

Singing, *YES JESUS LOVES ME ...O YES JESUS LOVES ME... YES JESUS LOVES ME ... FOR THE BIBLE TELLS ME SO.*

He loves you too beloved. My prayer is that above all things that you forgive yourself love yourself and be the best at being yourself because the role of being someone else is already taken.

LOVE YOU FOR REAL!
Apostle Julia D. Ford
"The General

And the Winner Is......

Apostle Julia Ford has a tremendous passion for God's word coupled with a love for God's people. She has a contagious spirit of generosity that flows through every facet of her ministry. Having received her mandate from God, Apostle Ford, obediently fulfills her calling God has on her life.

In 2002 Apostle Julia Ford was ordained as the first female minister at Resurrection Baptist Church (Philadelphia, PA). October 2009 under the leadership of Apostle Alexander Wm. Thompson, Ever Abundant Life Ministries (Darby, PA) Apostles Owen and Julia Ford, were "Sent Out" to begin the work known as True Love Church located in Folcroft, PA.

Apostle Julia is a dedicated vessel of God who thrives in excellence. Her goal is to make sure all of those that enter True Love Church experience the True Love of Christ.

www.ingramcontent.com/pod-product-compliance
Lightning Source LLC
Chambersburg PA
CBHW060434090426
42733CB00011B/2274